THE AUTHOR'S GUIDE TO EMAIL MARKETING

ROB EAGAR

The Author's Guide to
Email Marketing

Copyright © 2018 by Rob Eagar

Published by Wildfire Marketing
www.StartaWildfire.com

Requests to publish work from this book should be sent to:
Rob@Startawildfire.com

Cover design by Ron Dylnicki

❀ Created with Vellum

CONTENTS

ENDORSEMENTS

"I recommend Rob Eagar to any author looking to take their book campaign to a higher level."

Dr. Gary Chapman - #1 *New York Times* bestselling author of *The Five Love Languages*

"I give Rob Eagar my highest recommendation. If you want to increase book sales, make him the first person you hire."

Lysa TerKeurst - 4-time *New York Times* bestselling author

"Rob Eagar gets great results and strategically places authors in the right spaces. I'm happy with what Rob did for me, and I highly recommend him."

Dr. John Townsend - *New York Times* bestselling author of *Boundaries*

"Rob Eagar provided effective marketing strategy and worked closely with my team to execute new promotional ideas. I highly recommend Rob."

DeVon Franklin - CEO of Franklin Entertainment and *New York Times* bestselling author

"Rob Eagar knows how to use words and has fine penmanship. You should really listen to him."

His Mother - English major who taught Rob to speak clearly

"Rob revolutionized how I market my novels and connect with readers. His Book Marketing Master Class gave me more fantastic ideas than I knew what to do with."

Dani Pettrey - Bestselling novelist with over 300,000 copies sold

"Rob Eagar's expertise helped me develop a new brand and create an exciting new website. It was beyond my expectations and included everything I asked for and more."

Wanda Brunstetter - 6-time *New York Times* bestselling novelist with over 10 million copies sold

MY FREE GIFT FOR YOU

Get three e-books to help jumpstart your book sales for FREE:

Find Readers and Sell Books on a Shoestring Budget

Mastering Book Hooks for Authors

The Ultimate Book Marketing Plan Template for Authors

Join my email newsletter and get these three e-books. Each resource can be downloaded as a file to your computer or added to any e-reader device. You will also receive my weekly e-newsletter packed with free expert marketing advice for authors.

Download these three e-books for free today at:

https://www.startawildfire.com/free-ebooks-ag

PREFACE

If you've written a book, by definition you are considered an "author." Do you know what that title really means? Today, the word "author" means you are one of the bravest souls on the planet. Or, you might be one of the most unrealistic dreamers in our society. Why? Consider the incredible challenge that every modern author must face:

- Over 1,000,000 new books are published every year
- A book has less than a 1% chance of getting stocked on a bookstore shelf
- The average U.S. nonfiction book sells less than 250 copies per year

Source: https://www.bkconnection.com/the-10-awful-truths-about-book-publishing

With statistics like these, it's a wonder anyone decides to write a book. Yet, here you are. You're reading this guide because you're a writer seeking to beat the odds. You believe in yourself even though the numbers say success is nearly impossible. Or, you're just plain crazy, but crazy enough to follow your dreams.

Just like you, I chose to make a career out of writing books, even when my friends and family thought I had lost my mind. I entered the publishing world in 2002, before the luxury of fancy technology, such as social media, blogging, or live webcasts. Amazon was still a tiny company that no one thought would survive.

I'm also a maverick. I decided to self-publish my first book before it was cool to be an "indie" author. You could call me one of the original self-publishing success stories. I was just a normal guy who had never written a book, had no fan base, and had no idea what an "author platform" meant. However, I did possess a business education, 10 years of experience working in the corporate world, and a burning desire to share a message that I knew could help people.

Armed with headstrong determination, I tried every possible tactic to sell my books. I started small, but my persistence and hunger for marketing knowledge paid off. Within a few years, I sold over 13,000 copies on my own, built a nationwide following, and created an email list with over 8,000 subscribers. Public speaking was widely available at the time, so I spoke at over 170 events across North America to more than 35,000 people.

Equally important, I generated a six-figure income that allowed my wife to quit her job and join our business full-time. As my success grew, publishers began to court me with book contracts. I decided to trade-in my indie author hat and become a traditionally-published author. My self-published book was re-released with national distribution where it appeared in bookstores for over 10 years selling another 50,000 copies.

Did I hit any of the major bestseller lists? No, but I achieved something much more difficult. I figured out how to make a great living as an author and help other people through my writing, speaking, and spin-off products.

My success, however, led to an unexpected path. Authors began to seek me out for marketing advice. I was happy to share what I had learned. But, the distress calls became so frequent that I realized a need existed for expert information about marketing books. To meet this need, I started a consulting practice in 2007 called Wildfire Marketing.

To date, I've coached over 450 fiction and non-fiction authors. My client list includes numerous *New York Times* bestsellers, such as Dr. Gary Chapman, Dr. John Townsend, Dr. Harville Hendrix, Lysa TerKeurst, DeVon Franklin, and Wanda Brunstetter. In addition, I've provided consulting expertise to major publishers across the United States.

As new technology arrived, such as social media, online advertising, and the growth of Amazon, I studied how to use those digital tools to grow an author's book sales. I know what works and what is a waste of money.

As a consultant, I've helped first-time authors start out on the right foot. Plus, I've helped established authors achieve the highest levels of success. I also published my second book in 2012 with Writer's Digest called *Sell Your Book Like Wildfire*. However, due to constant changes in the publishing industry and technology, I chose to update and re-release all of my expertise in *The Author's Guide* book series that you're reading now.

Today, I work full-time teaching authors and publishers how to sell more books. It's my dream job, and I can't imagine doing anything else. But, I can't be everywhere at once, so I wrote this book to multiply my efforts and help instruct as many authors as possible.

I consider my background worth telling because it's imperative to take advice from someone who has achieved the same goal you seek. As the old adage says, "Never take financial guidance from a broke person." Likewise, don't take book marketing advice from someone who has never written a book or succeeded at selling their work. The publishing industry is filled with the "blind leading the blind." Instead, follow a leader who has already gone before you, knows the difference between the landmines and shortcuts, and has the experience to help you navigate a successful path.

This book was written to serve as your personal guide to help you sell more books. In the coming pages, I will dispel a lot of myths and offer a lot of new ideas. However, the information will have no benefit unless you're willing to work at marketing your book. You cannot spend one hour a week on promotional activities and expect your sales to grow. If you want to reach more readers, marketing should become synonymous with your writing. Engage in both activities throughout the course of your week and month.

I named my consulting practice "Wildfire Marketing," because I want to help you light a fire under your books, get them in front of more people, and enjoy the response of happy readers. When that happens, I hope you'll share your success story with me. That's the kind of tale I enjoy reading the most!

Rob Eagar

Wildfire Marketing

http://www.RobEagar.com

INTRODUCTION

I can tell within 30 seconds if an author is skilled at email marketing or not. How can I be so sure? I visit an author's website and observe what appears at the top of their home page. If I don't see an offer for free content in exchange for my email address, then I know that author doesn't realize the true power of email marketing. It only takes 30 seconds to search for any author's website on Google, examine their home page, and make my determination. It's that simple.

Would you pass or fail my 30-second test?

Authors who don't focus on building their email list miss out on one of the best ways to sell more books. Frankly, they miss out on the best opportunity to build their author career. There is no better way to ensure future success than growing a large email list. Not only will it help sell more books, a big email list will help you sell more of everything!

You may wonder why I don't base my 30-second test on the type of emails that an author sends to subscribers. That's because any author can send an email. Building a list is the hard part. In addition, few authors understand the nuance of sending emails that drive book sales. When you know how to get more subscribers and send effective emails campaigns, you will naturally sell more books.

Here's what you will learn in *The Author's Guide to Email Marketing*:

1. Proof email marketing is superior to social media
2. How to build a large email list
3. How to send emails that drive book sales

There are occasions throughout this book where I will provide links to resources and companies that might be helpful. To be clear, I do not receive any commission or revenue from these links. They are just my recommendations for you to explore and decide if they are a good fit for your needs.

Before we begin, here's how I suggest using this book to get the best results:

- Read the entire book first to get the big picture.
- Don't try to do everything at once or you'll wind up overwhelmed.
- Do not compare yourself to other authors that I mention or you'll get distracted.
- Decide on one key priority to make your focus for the next 30 – 90 days.

- Experience a quick short-term result and build upon that success.
- Don't expect overnight miracles. None of my *New York Times* bestselling clients are overnight successes. Each author worked for years to reach the highest level.

Let's get started. There is a lot of great information that I'm excited to share with you!

1

WHY EMAIL MARKETING WORKS

Let's begin with a pop quiz. Test your marketing acumen by correctly answering the following questions:

1. Social media is a better way to sell books than email. True or False?

2. Social media costs less than email. True or False?

3. More people see a social media post than read an email. True or False?

Like many authors, you many have answered all of the above questions as "True." Or, you might have answered true for one or two of the questions. Yet, the correct answer for all three questions is "False."

Email marketing is vastly superior to social media at selling books. I know you might be thinking, "Wait, email? Isn't it outdated? I thought Facebook is the best way to sell more books." I understand why this confusion occurs.

Many authors think selling books to their own social media fans will be easy. Instead, the opposite happens, because those same authors forget how social media works:

You can have thousands of social media followers. But, if you don't have thousands of social media RECOMMENDERS, then you won't sell many books.

Social media is designed to be a "social" system that works when you get hundreds of recommenders to tell their friends about your book. Good luck getting hundreds of other people to become your online sales force on Facebook or Twitter.

Unless you are a superstar author with a rabid following, you must borrow the social media platforms from a lot of other people who agree to market your book for you. That's a tall order for any author to pull off. Worse, the positive effect from borrowing other people's platforms only lasts for a short time. How do you consistently market your books to readers over a long period of time that produces results?

Repeated research has shown that email is vastly superior to social media at marketing books directly to an author's tribe of readers. If this reality should change and email becomes inferior, believe me, I'll drop email marketing like a hot rock and tell you to do the same. Until that happens, you need to know the facts.

A 2014 study by McKinsey Consulting stated that email

marketing was 40 times better at acquiring new customers than all social media combined.

A 2017 report by Custora examined data from dozens of top e-commerce retailers to reveal the primary channels that acquire online sales. Their study found that email was 12 times more powerful (18.5% versus 1.5%) than social media at generating new orders. Plus, the report showed that email trended higher over 2015 to 2016 while social media trended worse.

My own research with author clients reached the same conclusions. For example, I worked with a female author who has over 1,000,000 Facebook followers. Another client is a male author who has over 500,000 Facebook followers. When both authors launched their new books, we tracked the results and were shocked by the findings. In both cases, less than 1% of Facebook followers purchased a copy!

As you can imagine, these authors were disheartened by the pitiful Facebook response, especially after the time and money they invested to cultivate those fans. In addition, one of my publishing house clients has over 1,000,000 followers on their company Facebook page. They also confessed that very few book sales could be attributed to that audience.

These disappointments explain the hidden truth about social media. You can have all the followers in the world. But, if you don't have a lot of recommenders, then social media won't generate many book sales. Therefore, how do you sell a lot of books to your own following by yourself?

My experience working with authors and publishers has

found that email marketing regularly outperforms social media. For instance, I coached an author named Lysa TerKeurst who has an email list with over 900,000 subscribers. It took her over 10 years to reach that amount, but she consistently stayed with the process. To date, Lysa's huge email following has enabled her to hit the *New York Times* bestseller list four times in a row!

The power of email marketing can also help boost sales of older backlist books. For example, email helped me revive interest in a 23-year-old backlist book called *Boundaries* and get it onto the *New York Times* bestseller list. Even though the book had been in print for over two decades, it didn't get on that bestseller list until we built an email list with over 50,000 subscribers.

In addition, I read an interesting story about the successful business author, Dan Pink. He challenged his team to develop a way to hit the bestseller lists without having to spend huge money on expensive publicity firms. Dan's team found email was the best solution. As of this writing, Dan has over 150,000 email subscribers and recently hit the *New York Times* bestseller list for the fourth time with his book entitled, *When: The Scientific Secrets of Perfect Timing.*

Email marketing also works for indie or self-published authors, meaning those who handle all of the writing, distribution, and marketing functions on their own. Mark Dawson, author of the popular John Milton action thriller series, is one of the most successful indie novelists in the world. He swears by email marketing and has a list with over 80,000 subscribers. Those subscribers have bought and downloaded millions of Mark's books.

I could go on. Do you get my point? Authors who sell a lot of books directly to their fans use email marketing as their sales weapon of choice.

6 Reasons Why Email Is Superior to Social Media

The idea that email could outperform social media is a bitter pill for some people to swallow. They just can't believe that something invented in the 1970's could be better than something invented in the 2004. Maybe we want Facebook to work because it was originally offered as a way to unite the world for free. Emotional attachments to social media can be hard to overcome. If you fall into that category, let's examine six logical reasons why email is superior to social media at marketing books to your audience:

1. The vast majority of people still check their email several times a day.

When you send emails to a large list, you know people will receive it. Sure, not everyone will open your message. But, emails are always available to be seen, and typical open rates are 15% – 35%.

2. Facebook only allows 5% – 15% of followers to see a free post that you send.

The other 85% - 95% of your fans never see your free posts. That's a huge loss in audience reach. The only way to get Facebook to show a post to all of your followers is to pay for a sponsored post or a boosted post. That's an expensive proposition with no end in sight.

3. Most email lists contain less fake followers than social media.

Every email list contains some fake email addresses that people use just to get free stuff. But, you can weed them out over time. However, most Facebook audiences contain a significant percentage of dead accounts and fake users set up by hackers and fraudulent click farms. These fakers are nearly impossible to identify and remove.

4. You have no control over Facebook, Twitter, or other social media platforms.

They can change the rules or adjust their algorithms at any moment. However, you always have control over your email list. No one can change it or delete it.

5. Facebook could go out of style or get hacked.

Remember when MySpace and QR codes were all the rage? Today, they're the butt of nerd jokes. The same could eventually happen to Facebook or other platforms. Worse, every social media service is an enticing target for nefarious hackers. While I was writing this book, Facebook admitted that attackers entered their system and gained control of nearly 50 million accounts! The hackers were able to act as if they were the users in charge of those accounts. This is only the beginning. Hackers could eventually figure out how to access anyone's account and wipe out their audience. In contrast, your email list can never be destroyed as long as you regularly back it up.

6. Email only requires sending a few messages a month to be effective.

Email marketing is less time-consuming than social media. Email only requires sending a few messages per month to be effective. Whereas, social media requires sending several posts every day. Social media demands the focus of a full-time job, costs more money than email, and still yields worse results.

If these six reasons don't convince you that email is superior to social media, you're welcome to keep your head in the sand. But, you will miss out on the best way to sell more books. I have nothing against social media. I just want you to know what works best.

If you're ready to increase book sales, one of your top priorities should be to increase the size of your email list. For authors just starting out, I recommend setting an initial goal to reach 10,000 subscribers. That may sound like a big number, but it's possible to achieve over time. Let me help put your mind at ease in the next chapter by explaining how to grow your author email list for free.

2

ATTRACT EMAIL SUBSCRIBERS WITH CONTENT MAGNETS

Unless you're a celebrity or a well-known individual, very few people will join your email list out of the goodness of their heart. Everyone's email inbox is already filled with messages and junk mail. People need an attractive reason to join your email list. The secret to building a large email list is to give people enticing incentives.

If you just put a boring box on your author website that says, "Join My Email List" or "Sign Up for News and Updates," good luck getting many subscribers. However, if you give away free e-books, a video course, a novella, or some short stories, you can dramatically improve your email signup rate. I like to call these types of incentives "content magnets."

A "content magnet" is a piece of free content given away to magnetically attract email subscribers. Your goal is to offer material that people would be surprised to get for free. You know a content magnet is effective when people respond,

"Wow, I can't believe you gave this material away for free. It's substantial enough that I would have paid for it."

To be clear, a content magnet is not a sample chapter from your book, a makeshift collection of blog posts, or outdated teaching lessons. A content magnet needs to satisfy as a standalone piece of material. If your content magnet fails to impress, then people will view it as a sneaky promotion or a bait-and-switch tactic.

The easiest way to create a content magnet is to select a portion of the best material that you've written. What qualifies as your best content? The answer to that question usually lies in the material that has received the most positive audience response. Select that material as your content magnet. Don't worry about giving away the farm or losing your shirt. The more generous you are with your best material, the greater response you will receive.

As of this writing, I give away three free e-books on my website as my content magnets. The e-books are concise, but some of my best instruction. Ever since I became more generous and offered multiple e-books, my email signup rate tripled.

If you're a first-time author, here's a bold suggestion: give away your entire book as your content magnet. Yes, I just said to give away the whole thing for free. Before you throw this book across the room, listen to me. You can give your book away and still make money. How? Keep selling your book on Amazon and the other retailers.

Readers on Amazon will never know that you're giving away

the book for free on your website. So, they'll still buy your book. People who visit your author website will join your email list, because they can't believe you're giving away an entire book for free. If those people like your free book, then you'll get more Amazon reviews and more word of mouth. Most importantly, when your second book is ready to launch, you'll have a much bigger email list to drive more sales.

However, if you simply cannot stomach the idea of giving away an entire book for free, consider these other options for effective content magnets:

Options for Fiction Content Magnets:

- Give away an entire e-book (ha, I said it again)
- Write a prequel novella tied to your novel
- Assemble a collection of short stories
- Create a compilation sampler with the first three chapters of all your novels

Options for Non-Fiction Content Magnets:

- Develop a concise teaching guide with material from one or more books
- Create a 7-day or 30-day challenge using content pulled from a book
- Create a free video course based on material from your book
- Turn material from your book into a daily devotional or bite-sized guide

- Offer a sampler or compilation of the best material from several books
- Give away an entire e-book (yes, I said it a third time)

To help you spark additional ideas, the next two sections describe actual examples of content magnets for non-fiction and fiction authors.

Examples of Content Magnets for Non-Fiction Authors

When I consulted with *New York Times* bestselling author, DeVon Franklin, we created different types of content magnets based on his various books. For his business book, *The Hollywood Commandments*, we turned material from the manuscript into a PDF download called "The 5 Unwritten Rules to Win at Work." We highlighted this free offer on DeVon's website and his social media pages. Within 3 months, this resource attracted over 4,000 new email subscribers for free.

In addition, we created a second content magnet based on DeVon's bestselling relationship book, *The Wait*. Using material from this manuscript, we developed a content magnet called "The Unwritten Rules to Dating and Waiting." Within 60 days, over 10,000 people joined DeVon's email list to get that free PDF download. That's what I call the power of a content magnet!

Another client named Jeremie Kubicek writes books that help people improve their leadership skills. I worked with Jeremie and his team to develop an online assessment based on his book called *The 5 Voices: How to Communicate with Everyone You Lead.* On Jeremie's book website, he offered this free assessment to help visitors identify their personal leadership strengths. At live events, he promoted the free tool at his resource booth. To receive the assessment results, people provided their email address and the information was sent to their inbox. This content magnet helped Jeremie attract over 3,000 new email subscribers within the first 6 weeks.

Examples of Content Magnets for Novelists

Indie science fiction author, Chris Fox, gives away three complete e-books as content magnets to build his email list, including *Exiled, The First Ark,* and *Planetstrider.* You might think giving away so many books would hurt his sales potential. Instead, the opposite reaction occurs. Chris' generous approach allowed him to build an email list much faster than giving away short excerpts or small samples. Many of those email subscribers turned into serial readers. In turn, they buy a lot of Chris' other books and allow him to enjoy a six-figure income as a writer.

One of my *New York Times* bestselling clients, Wanda Brunstetter, writes popular novels set in the Amish country. (Don't laugh at the Amish genre...Wanda has sold over 10 million copies.) To attract more email subscribers, Wanda created a free e-book of 30 mouthwatering Amish recipes as a content magnet. She and her publisher promoted her free recipe e-book on their websites and grew Wanda's email list by 75% within seven months.

Obviously, these case studies represent incredible results. But, I purposefully selected these examples to show you what is possible. Not every author will grow their email list this fast. But, you won't grow your list if you don't offer an enticing incentive. Since content magnets are free to create, what have you got to lose?

Your Title Will Determine Your Sign-Up Success

When you offer people a content magnet to join your email list, keep this rule of thumb in mind:

> *People aren't attracted to your content magnet.*
> *They are attracted to the title.*

Put yourself in the shoes of someone visiting your website. They don't know that you really want them to join your email list. They're just surfing your website to see if anything looks interesting. They never see or think about a "content magnet." That's just a nerdy term that I created to explain your email signup incentive.

Therefore, people will only respond if the title of your content magnet seems appealing. No one can view the material you're giving away until after they join your email list. So, they are taking a risk to hope your content magnet will be worth the exchange of their email address.

From the reader's perspective, you're not offering a content magnet. You are offering a title. Thus, your content magnet title must be persuasive. Otherwise, all the work you do to create your content magnet could be wasted. Below are tips you can use to create effective titles:

Tips to Create Fiction Content Magnet Titles:

1. If offering a prequel connected to a novel, create a title similar to the original book to show the connection between the two items.

2. Use emotional language to explain what people will feel when reading your content magnet, such as "3 Breathless Romance Reads" or "The Haunting Trilogy."

3. If offering a compilation, use a number in the title to display how many stories you are giving away, such as "6 Short Stories to Keep You Up All Night."

4. I'll say it again. Offering an entire book as your content magnet is a safe bet for novelists. It's very effective to say "Free Book," and then you can use the title of your book.

Tips to Create Non-Fiction Content Magnet Titles:

1. Define the problem that your material addresses and include that problem in the content magnet title.

2. Use a different version of your book title for the content magnet. For example, Charles Duhigg converted his best-selling book title, *The Power of Habit*, into several content magnets with similar titles, such as "A Guide to Changing Habits" and a cool video called, "How Habits Works." See details at: https://charlesduhigg.com/additional-resources/

3. Use attention-grabbing words and phrases in your title to entice interest, such as:

The Ultimate Guide to...

How to...

The Top 10... or 10 Reasons...

Secrets of...

5 Steps to...

The Unwritten Rules of...

The 7-Day Challenge...

For example, I worked with *New York Times* bestselling author, Dr. Harville Hendrix, who appeared on Oprah's television program 17 times as a relationship expert. When he needed ideas for content magnets to build his email list, we developed these four provocative titles:

How to Make Love All the Time and Enjoy Sex Too

Secrets Men Don't Tell Their Wives

How to Have a Fight-Free Relationship

The Happy Couple's Secret

People loved these titles, and they created the desired results. Within the first 120 days, these four e-books attracted over 1,500 new email subscribers and were downloaded over 5,000 times.

The Magic Question to Create Effective Content Magnets

Choosing the right type of content magnet is vital to growing your email list. But, here's an even better tip to ensure you get more email subscribers. If you feel uncertain about the type of content magnet that would appeal to your audience, ask them the "magic question."

The magic question is an excellent insight from Jeff Walker in his *New York Times* bestselling book, *Launch*, which I highly recommend. In his book, Jeff explains how the following question helps determine the free resource that people will naturally find appealing. The magic question is:

Tell me your biggest challenge as it relates to ...

Why is this question so powerful? The answer you receive tells you exactly what people want and what they are willing to buy. For example, I posed this question in a survey that I sent to over 500 authors by asking:

Tell me your biggest challenge as it relates to book marketing...

As a so-called expert, I thought I knew the top answer. I was sure most authors would say, "selling more books on Amazon" or "understanding social media." Instead, I was blind-sided by the most common response. The majority of authors replied that their biggest book marketing challenge was "finding new readers." Duh! How could I miss something so basic and important? Authors can't sell more books unless they figure out how to find new readers.

I might have missed the obvious, but I'm no dummy. Armed with the answer to the magic question, I quickly created a new e-book content magnet called *Find New Readers and Sell Books on a Shoestring Budget*. Immediately after I started offering this content magnet on my website, my email signup response rate improved. That's because I was no longer guessing what people wanted from me. I asked them to tell me what they wanted and created a content magnet to meet their need.

As an aside, this magic question can also help you identify the next book to write, the next product to launch, or the next service to create. Don't beat your head against the wall trying to read people's minds. Do the opposite. Let people tell you what they want to buy from you.

Make Your Content Magnet Look Professional

An effective content magnet needs more than just a persuasive title and satisfying material. If the artwork looks unprofessional, your results can suffer. If you give away an e-book or a novella, make the investment to create a professional-looking cover image for your content magnet.

If there's one marketing mistake that too many authors make, it's settling for crummy artwork. Why shoot yourself in the foot? I know budget-conscious authors who ask their nephew, neighbor, or an amateur designer to create artwork for their material. It usually ends up with a home-made look. But, they reason that it's just a freebie, so its good enough. Then, those same authors wonder why few people show interest in their content magnet. Leave the amateurs alone, or you'll wind up looking like the amateur yourself.

We live in a visual, online world where people make decisions based on the what they see on a computer screen. Your content magnet is one of your most important marketing assets. You want the cover to look as professional as the cover for your regular books. First impressions make a difference.

If necessary, hire a trained graphic artist to design a cover for you. It's doesn't need to look extravagant, just professional. In my experience, graphic artists tend to respond best when you show them examples of what you want. It may be necessary to educate them on the goals of your content magnet and provide examples or instruction to follow. For example, these tips have helped my clients obtain good cover art from designers:

- Use similar artwork or text fonts from your regular book covers
- Show your graphic artist pictures of other covers you like and ask them to mimic those designs
- Look at the top-selling books in your category on Amazon's website and pull design elements from those successful books
- Show a designer pictures of content magnets from other successful authors

If you don't know where to find a professional graphic artist who designs book covers or you prefer the do-it-yourself path, try inexpensive services, such as Canva or Reedsy.

Canva is an online service that provides free samples and templates of book covers you can select. Their system is based on a drag-and-drop format and provides access to over a million photographs, graphics, and fonts. You don't have to be a professional to use their website. Plus, their tools can be used for both web designs and print media designs. For details, visit: https://www.canva.com

Reedsy is an international online community of publishing professionals who offer freelance skills that you can hire for specific projects, such as cover design and editing. Many of the professionals have industry experience working for major publishing houses and creating bestselling book covers. Plus, you can view samples of a designer's portfolio to find someone who is the right fit for your genre and specific needs. For details, visit: https://Reedsy.com

Once your content magnet has a great-looking cover and is ready to launch, the easiest way to provide it to the public is via a downloadable PDF file. PDF files can be read on any computer, smartphone, or tablet device. I typically create my content magnets using Microsoft Word, add the cover image to the first page, then save it as a PDF file.

If your content magnet is a video or audio file, you can upload it to YouTube, Vimeo, or SoundCloud and set the file to private. Then, embed those links onto a page on your author website for viewing. Or, you can email the link to your new subscribers within a "welcome email."

Here's another tech tip: If you want to make an e-book content magnet available on all e-reader devices, such as the Kindle, Nook, or iPad tablets, I recommend an inexpensive service called Book Funnel. Their technology enables any author to offer an e-book file in every format necessary to be read on any e-reader device in existence. Plus, they handle all of the system updates, provide reporting features to track the downloads, and manage all customer service issues. Visit their website at: http://www.BookFunnel.com

Don't Ride a Dead Content Magnet

You may be familiar with the idiom, "Don't beat a dead horse," which means don't waste time and effort trying to do something impossible. This adage also applies to your content magnet. For our usage, I would adjust the idiom to say, "Don't ride a dead content magnet," which means don't waste time with a content magnet that fails to produce consistent results.

If you create a content magnet that doesn't grow your email list, then you must kill that content magnet and try something else. I cannot overemphasize this point enough. No matter how much you like your content magnet, get rid of it if other people don't like it. All that matters are the results.

Typically, you get one shot to convert people who visit your website into email subscribers. If that initial attempt fails, don't blame your website visitors – blame your content magnet. Building your list is far too important to rely on an under-performing or dead content magnet. Take the content magnet out behind the barn, shoot it, and ride something new.

If you're wondering how to judge whether your content

magnet is successful and gauge proper signup rates, I'll answer that question in the next chapter.

An effective content magnet should produce good results for a long time, such as many months and even a few years. For instance, novelists who give away free e-books can leave those offers running for a long time. Most people who visit an author website are first-time visitors, so they've never seen the content magnet before. It appears new in their eyes, which keeps the appeal fresh over lengthy period.

However, it's time to change your content magnet if you notice email sign-up rates consistently declining. For example, let's say you average 100 new subscribers per week for several months. If that number drops to 50 – 60 per week for a month or two, then you know the content magnet is growing stale. It's probably time to create something new that gets a better conversion rate.

The numbers don't lie. Track your email sign-up rate using the free reports provided by your email service provider. Their statistics can quickly tell you if the rate of new subscribers is growing or trending downwards. That way, you can make an educated decision, rather than an emotional guess.

Now that you've got good ideas to create an effective content magnet, let's talk about how to display it on your website and get the world's attention.

3

TURN YOUR WEBSITE INTO A SIGN-UP MACHINE

If you have an author website, which option below represents the best way to grow your book sales?

A. Design your website to focus on selling books.

B. Design your website to focus on building your email list.

Option B is the correct answer, even though it may sound counterintuitive. At first glance, designing your website to focus on selling books may seem logical. Every author wants to sell more books. But, here's the problem with that decision. If someone comes to your website and doesn't make a purchase, they will likely never return in the future. Website statistics, such as Google Analytics, typically show that you get just one chance to connect with a new reader.

That's why Option B is a wiser choice than Option A. Design your website to focus on building your email list. If someone visits your author website, doesn't buy a book, but they join your email list – it is okay if they never return to your website. You can market your books to that person in the future via your email list.

Take the long-term view. Don't focus on the quick sale. Concentrate on capturing email signups so that your list steadily builds over time. When you maintain this perspective, you will wind up with a much larger list to help successfully launch every new book you write. Plus, you'll have a bigger audience to market your backlist.

Make email signups the number one goal of your website. Selling books is priority number two. I know you might be thinking, "Rob just spoke heresy! I need the book sales right now," or "My publisher will think I'm crazy for switching priorities." Trust me, you will be fine.

Arrange your website home page to draw visual attention to your content magnet offer. People generally buy what is presented to them upfront and often. This same truth applies to email signups. You must present the opportunity for people to join your list by clearly promoting your content magnet and making the opportunity easy to see.

In the previous chapter, I gave several examples of helping my author clients rapidly grow their email lists. One of the secrets to success is placing four email signup opportunities on the author's website home page, including:

1. A dedicated section at the top of the home page to promote the content magnet.

2. A pop-up window appears after a 10-second delay offering the content magnet.

3. A permanent link to join the author's email list above the site navigation bar.

4. A permanent link to join the author's email list in the website footer section.

Why do I load up the home page with multiple ways to get email sign-ups? Every author's home page is typically the most visited page on the entire site. The vast majority of visitors will only come to the home page, look around for a bit, and then leave. Why risk letting them get away without joining your email list? Make your content magnet offer the first item they see.

Another secret to success is using persuasive language to promote your content magnet. I suggest displaying text that lets people know you're being generous, because in truth, you are being generous. Offering a content magnet is being strategically charitable. You are giving free material in order to get an email address in return. Use phrases to promote the generosity of your content magnet to website visitors, such as:

My free gift for you...

I want to give you this...

Join my email list for free e-books...

I'd like to give you 3 free e-books...

When you appear as a generous-minded author giving away great content for free, people are more apt to respond. Getting someone's email is a privilege. Treat people with respect by acknowledging their skepticism and offering your content magnet as a substantial gift. (I'm assuming your truly being generous and not hoarding your best material.)

A note about pop-up windows mentioned at #2 on the list above. Pop-ups can be a controversial idea with varying opinions. Some people are against using pop-up windows on websites, because they can be considered annoying. Some say Google may penalize websites that employ pop-ups. In my work with clients, though, I've found tasteful pop-up windows to be an effective way to present enticing content magnets.

Interrupting people on my website with pop-up offers for my content magnet increased traffic to my sign-up page by 5% – 10%. Plus, pop-ups are the best way to make sure people know that your content magnet exists. It's a personal choice, though. Use pop-up windows and interrupter technology at your discretion.

The bottom line is that if you downplay your content magnet to the point website visitors don't see it, then you will get a low response rate. Make your top priority obvious to your website visitors. Invite them to join your email list.

Convert Visitors Into Subscribers With a Landing Page

Once people express an interest in your free content magnet, what do you do next? Display a button or a link on your home page that sends them to a landing page to complete the transaction and capture their email address.

A "landing page" is a specific page on your website where people "land" and are persuaded to request your free content magnet. This dedicated page is meant to minimize distractions and display only an image of your content magnet, compelling marketing text, influential testimonials, and a field for people to enter the email address. In other words, you get people's attention for your content magnet on your home page, but you send them to a landing page to close the deal and get the email address.

Once someone enters their email address into the signup form on your landing page, it is added to your email list automatically using code than connects to your email service provider (see details about email service providers in Chapter 4). When set up correctly, you have an automated system working in the background to secure new email subscribers while you're busy writing your next book.

Why drive people to a landing page? Isn't that an unnecessary step? There are logical reasons to use landing pages. First, most home pages and website subpages are cluttered with a navigation bar, numerous sections of text, and multiple links to other parts of the site. All of these choices can distract visitors who move on before joining your email list.

In addition, I'm not a fan of using tiny boxes on your home page to get email addresses. That's because those elements can be hard to use on small mobile device screens, which account for half of all website traffic. Instead, send people to a landing page designed to convert traffic into email subscribers.

On a landing page, you don't display any navigation options or links to other parts of your website. All visual distractions are stripped away so that website visitors can focus on your content magnet offer. It's a simplified page that shows only the following items:

- Picture of your content magnet that looks professional
- 300 – 500 words of persuasive marketing text
- Sign-up form for people to enter their email address
- Influential testimonials if you have them
- Link to your email privacy policy

Using landing pages makes it easier to track the performance of your content magnet and conversion rates. Free services, such as Google Analytics, help you trace how many people visit the page, where they come from, and how many join your email list. It's much more difficult to get that data if you use a signup box or a pop-up window embedded on your website home page.

Another side benefit of landing pages is that they can serve as the hub to send people from Facebook ads or other promotional campaigns you run. When someone clicks on your ad, you know they'll be directed to a page where you can control the process. However, I recommend creating separate landing pages for each of your ad campaigns in order to accurately track the performance of each promotion.

I know this part of the chapter may seem like I'm deep in

the weeds of technology. If you're confused about creating a landing page, follow this description of a high-converting landing pages that worked well for me:

1. Start the layout for your landing page at the top by displaying a short sentence in large font that says, "Join My Email Newsletter for Free e-Books, Updates, and Helpful Tips." If you write fiction, your landing page text could say, "Join My Mailing List for Updates and Free e-Books." Be sure to tell people up-front that they are joining your email list in order to prevent confusion and abide by current privacy and legal requirements.

2. Next, display a picture of your content magnet. If you give away free e-books, display the cover images for those books. If you give away a free video series or an audio download, display a thumbnail image of your video or an image that represents an audio file.

3. Below the image section, display one paragraph of marketing text that describes your content magnet and the benefits people will receive. Use a bulleted list to make the separate benefits easy to read.

4. Below the marketing text, display a few testimonials from influential people if you have them available. If not, you can skip this step.

5. Next, display the sign-up form for people to enter their email address along with a button that says, "Enter" or "Sign Up."

6. At the bottom of the landing page, be sure to mention your privacy policy to stay current with legal requirements.

For example, you could display text that says, "I will not spam or share your email address. You may opt out at any time. Read my privacy policy here." Then, provide a link to the privacy policy page on your website. For more details on legal issues, see Chapter 4.

Don't Forget to Say Thank You

When you were a child, it's likely you were taught to say "thank you" after someone gave you a present. Those proper manners also apply in the online world. After people give you their email address to receive your content magnet, complete the transaction by telling them "thank you." Don't leave people hanging, wondering what to do next or you can appear unprofessional.

There are different schools of thoughts regarding how to say "thank you" and deliver your content magnet to people. Some marketers suggest displaying a short thank you message, but make people wait to receive an automated "welcome email" with a link to access the content magnet. There is nothing wrong with using this approach.

In my opinion, however, most people who join your email list would rather not wait or take extra steps to receive your content magnet. I believe the best way to deliver your content magnet is by using a "thank you" page on your website that provides two pieces of information:

1. A link to access the content magnet(s) you're offering

2. A brief description of what to expect from you by email in the future

A "thank you page" is a simple website page automatically connected to your landing page described earlier. When someone enters their email address into the form on your landing page and clicks on the "enter" button, then a "thank you page" should automatically appear. This time-saving step allows people to immediately enjoy the free content magnet that you worked so hard to make appealing.

If you're giving away free e-books as your content magnet, you can also use third-party services, such as BookFunnel, to create your "thank you" page and deliver the e-book files to new subscribers. BookFunnel is inexpensive and ensures that your e-books can be easily read on any e-reader device on the planet. For more details, visit:

http://www.BookFunnel.com

Let's Get Technical

The idea of creating landing pages and thank you pages may cause your head to spin. If you're challenged by technology, here are some options to consider based on your skill level:

1. Do you know how to use Wordpress or HTML code?

It's easy to set up a landing page by yourself. Simply create a new page on your website, give it a unique name, turn off the navigation and footer sections, paste in the details about your content magnet, link to your privacy policy, and insert an email signup field.

I recommend automatically adding someone's email

address to your list, rather than wasting time to do it manually. To automate the process, you can get code to add an email registration form from your email service provider (see details about email service providers in Chapter 4). That code enables you to make a sign-up form appear on your landing page that directly connects to your email list. However, you will need to make sure the code includes a command to show people the "thank you" page after they enter their information.

If your website uses the Wordpress platform, there are inexpensive software plug-ins, such as Gravity Forms (https://www.gravityforms.com/), that enable you to set up professional sign-up forms on your landing page. In addition, Gravity Forms lets you automate the "confirmation" step by sending new email subscribers directly to your thank you page. In the confirmation settings, just insert the URL address to that specific page.

2. Do you have a webmaster who manages your website?

Ask him or her to create a landing page and thank you page for your content magnet. This is the easiest option and should be inexpensive. It takes a skilled webmaster only a few hours of billable work to set everything up for you. However, give your webmaster my list of necessary items described above to ensure your landing page maximizes results.

3. Are you uncomfortable using HTML code and no access to a webmaster?

Use a third-party service to create a landing page for your

content magnet. There are numerous online services that offer pre-created templates to create landing pages and thank you pages on your own.

For example, Weebly (http://www.Weebly.com) is online service that lets you create landing pages for free using their system. The "catch" is that their free system includes advertising for their company at the bottom of the page. But, that's a fair trade-off to get a landing page at no cost.

There are also paid services, such as LeadPages (http://www.Leadpages.net), which specialize in providing easy-to-use templates to create landing pages. Their service isn't cheap, but they offer a lot of templates that have been rigorously tested for better performance. Plus, their templates will connect directly to your email service provider and automatically add new subscribers to your list.

If you choose the third-party route, keep in mind that the URL link for your landing page may not include your author website address. Instead, the landing page will reside on the third-party servers and use their company URL address. That's okay, most people visiting your author website don't care about specific URL addresses. They just want to see your content magnet displayed in a professional manner that looks trustworthy.

Realistic Email Signup Rates

The time has come to answer the $100,000 question, "If you offer people an enticing content magnet, how many new email subscribers should you expect to receive?" The answer depends on a variety of factors. Sorry, I know that sounds like an evasive response, but it's the truth.

There are numerous elements that can affect your email sign-up success rate. For instance, if you get a lot of traffic to your author website or have a large social media following, it's easy to convert a percentage of those people into email subscribers.

For instance, when I consult with bestselling authors who have a large platform, they typically add 100 – 1,000 new email subscribers per week. Those well-known authors generate so much exposure that they can consistently promote their content magnet to a lot of people. Even if their conversion rate is only 5% – 10%, that's a lot of new subscribers at a rapid pace.

On the other hand, if an author's audience is small, it may be realistic to expect only 50 – 100 new email subscribers per month. The ability to secure new subscribers is largely dependent on how many people visit your author website. If the traffic is low, then it's possible to buy online advertising to reach a wider audience (I'll discuss advertising a content magnet in the last section of this chapter.)

If you are expecting to grow your email list overnight, be wary of falling into a "get rich quick" mentality. Consider how financial planners give retirement advice. For example, if you want to retire someday with one million dollars in the bank, you don't achieve that goal by getting rich quick. Most people retire as millionaires by consistently growing their savings over time. They start with a small amount, invest it wisely, and continue adding more money over the years.

Their consistent focus pays off with a comfortable life in the future.

The same principle applies to building your email list. I've never met an author who went from zero to 100,000 subscribers in a year. Sure, it may be possible. But, growing your email list takes time and consistent focus. If you stick with the process by offering appealing content magnets, your list will grow at a steady pace.

One of my most successful clients has over 1,000,000 email subscribers. But, it took her 10 years to reach that number. With a list that large, though, this author is in a constant position of strength. She routinely hits the *New York Times* bestseller list and makes a lot of money. The size of her list puts a whole new spin on being a millionaire.

If You Offer It, They Will Join

It's fun to dream about having a big email list. But, what if you're just getting started? Or, what if you don't receive much traffic to your author website? If few people visit your website, how can you get more subscribers at a rapid rate? Flip the script. If people don't come to you, then go to them.

Identify where your audience congregates in large numbers, then pursue opportunities to promote your content magnet to those big groups. Some options can be free. Some options will require spending money. First, let's consider several options that are free:

Free options to attract more email subscribers:

1. Free social media posts

If you're active on social media, create free posts that promote your content magnets. Not everyone will see your free posts, but it doesn't cost a dime to recruit email subscribers from your social media platforms.

2. Partner with influencers

Partner with other authors or influencers to ask if they will promote your content magnet to their audience. Be prepared to promote their content magnet in return for the favor. A partnership usually involves taking the same actions for each other.

3. Media interviews

If you land a radio or TV interview, mention your content magnet offer and author website address during your interview. This is one of the easiest techniques to add a lot of new subscribers in a short time for free. But, you must have the guts to turn a media interview into building your email list, rather than wasting a golden opportunity.

4. Create an Amazon "Bait Book"

Create a free "bait book" on Amazon and attract email subscribers from their huge audience. For details on this advanced technique, see my book, *The Author's Guide to Marketing Books on Amazon*.

5. Public speaking

If you speak in public or conduct an author book-signing event, use those opportunities to grow your list. Tell everyone in the room about your free content magnet and ask them to sign up. Since you're face-to-face with people, your appeal can be quite compelling. Make it easy for people to join your list by providing slips of paper for people to write their email address. Or, use a computer or tablet device to let people enter their email electronically.

For example, when I wrote my first book in 2002, public speaking was an excellent option to grow my email list for free. As I spoke in front of audiences, I used to give away a giant chocolate candy bar as part of my presentation. I told everyone listening that if they joined my free email newsletter, I would enter their name into a drawing to win the huge candy bar at the end of the event. Since my offer was so appealing, the response was incredible. In most cases, over 80% of the audience willingly joined my email list. That technique helped me grow my first email list from zero to 8,000 subscribers in a couple of years.

Paid options to attract more email subscribers:

Beside the five free methods previously described, you can also spend money to build your email list. If you have the budget available, there are additional ways to grow your email list at a fast pace. Just make sure to calculate your cost of acquisition so that you don't lose money in the process.

The following two paid options can be a wise investment when used with prudence:

1. Buy ads on someone else's large email list.

Some authors and organizations with big email lists offer affordable advertising opportunities that authors can purchase. In my experience, ad rates can run anywhere from $50 - $3,000. The ad price is usually determined by the size of the email list. Buying ad space on a list with 500,000 subscribers will cost more than purchasing an ad on a list with 50,000 subscribers.

Two benefits to buying ad space on another author's email list include the ability to reach a large targeted audience and be endorsed by the author selling the ad. If you don't get many visitors to your author website, someone else's large email list gives you access to a huge new source of traffic. Plus, some advertising opportunities will include a recommendation of your book to the audience and provide third-party credibility. Therefore, you'll get a higher response rate due to being "endorsed" by that author.

For example, I helped an author client purchase a "guest article" that appeared on another author's large email newsletter with over 500,000 subscribers. The topic of the guest article was pulled from the material in my client's book. The cost to place the article was $3,000. But, the price included an endorsement from the owner of the email list. At the end of the article, a link was displayed that promoted my client's free content magnet and join his email list.

The results were impressive. Within 72 hours after the

"guest article" appeared, over 6,000 people joined my client's email list. Not only did this response quickly grow my client's list, but the cost of acquisition was only $.50 per subscriber ($3,000 ad price / 6,000 new subscribers = $.50 cost of acquisition). Anytime you can add new email subscribers for less than $1.00 per person, you're getting a great deal.

If you'd like to buy advertising space on another email list to promote your content magnet, search for opportunities with the top authors or industry groups in your specific genre. Your goal is to attract new subscribers who are the right fit for your book. For instance, if you write science fiction novels, it would be a waste of money to buy ad space on an email list dedicated to fans of romance stories.

Regardless of your genre, there are typically bestselling authors or industry groups with large email lists that offer advertising opportunities. Visit their websites and look for links that say, "Advertise with Us" or "Advertising Rates." Here's a sample of advertising opportunities for three specific genres:

If you write romantic fiction, there are affordable ad options with the Romance Writers of America trade association. For details, visit: http://www.rwa.org

If you write thriller novels, there is advertising available with the International Thriller Writers organization. For details, visit: http://thrillerwriters.org

If you write religious non-fiction, check out advertising

opportunities at Christianity Today. For details, visit: http://www.christianitytoday.com

2. Buy Facebook ads to promote your content magnet.

If you're adept at buying Facebook ads for your book, you can also use their platform to advertise your free content magnet. For example, if you write espionage fiction similar to Daniel Silva or self-help non-fiction similar to Brene Brown, you can target their fans on Facebook. Their fans make likely candidates to appreciate your content magnet and join your email list.

However, buying Facebook ads can be a complicated process that has a bit of a learning curve. There isn't enough space in this book to cover all of the details. If you're interested learning about Facebook ads, I suggest reviewing their free online training material called Facebook Blueprint at: https://www.facebook.com/blueprint

Regarding budget, Facebook ads usually cost at least $500 - $1,000 per month to generate effective results. Your goal is to get as many email signups for the money you spend. There are some authors who report adding people to their email list for less than $1.00 per person. Other authors say they pay $5.00 or more per new subscriber. It usually involves a lot of trial and error to maximize the return on investment. Fortunately, Facebook provides affordable daily budget limits, such as $10 per day along with real-time reporting data. If you monitor the statistics they provide, you can adjust your budget to avoid paying more money than you are comfortable spending.

If you choose to buy Facebook ads to build your email list, I recommend creating two elements to accurately track the results. First, set up a separate landing page just for the people who click on your Facebook ad. That way, you can correctly measure how many people visit your email sign-up offer during the advertising campaign.

Second, when people join your email list from the landing page for your ad, set up a separate email list for those people, such as a list called "Facebook Ad Subscribers." By using these two steps together, you can accurately trace who joins your list from Facebook ads.

Judging the success of an advertising campaign is based on knowing exactly how many people take action based on your ad. Therefore, if you don't create the two elements listed above, a lot of confusion can be introduced into your tracking process. It would be a shame to pay for advertising but never know if the ad actually worked. Take these steps to ensure you accurately calculate your return on investment.

Facebook ads aside, you should now feel confident that you can turn your author website into a sign-up machine and build your email list. In the next chapter, I'll answer several frustrating questions that plague authors about email marketing.

4

EMAIL MARKETING QUESTIONS THAT PLAGUE AUTHORS

Thus far, you understand why email marketing works and how any author can get people to join their email list. However, creating a content magnet and displaying it on your website doesn't mean everything will be easy. In my experience coaching hundreds of authors, there are several concerns that arise at this stage of the process. Below is a list of five common questions that plague authors about email:

- How do I choose a good email service provider?
- Should authors use a single or double opt-in email policy?
- What about privacy issues and new government regulations?
- What is a typical email open rate to expect?
- What if my email list isn't growing?

In this chapter, let's address these confusing questions and put your mind at ease.

How to Pick an Email Service Provider

If you are new to the concept email marketing, you may not be aware of the need to pay for an email service provider. Why pay someone else to send your emails? Two reasons: it would be highly time-consuming and unethical to send lots of emails to a large group of people directly from your own computer.

For instance, if you try sending a personal email to 1,000 people using your personal Gmail or Outlook account, your Internet service provider will flag you as a spammer. Sending spam emails can cause you to lose your Internet account and be subject to stiff fines from governments around the world (see Question #3 in this chapter for legal details).

If you want to avoid being labeled a spammer, how do you send a mass email to hundreds or thousands of subscribers on your list? More importantly, how do make sure your emails look professional and track the response rate from recipients? You use an inexpensive email service provider.

A good email service provider enables you to create nice-looking emails, manage your subscribers, and track the performance of your email campaigns. Above all, an email marketing service ensures that your emails don't wind up in people's spam folder.

At the time of this writing, there are dozens of email service providers on the market. But, three of the most popular companies among authors are MailChimp, Constant

Contact, and ConvertKit. Their pricing and features constantly change, so I won't waste time discussing details that could be obsolete in 6 months. However, let's take a quick look at each company to compare their differences and determine the right option for you.

MailChimp

MailChimp is arguably the most popular email service providers among authors. Their system provides a simple interface with great tools and excellent online support. Plus, their service is easy to integrate with WordPress and other website platforms. In addition, they tend to be on the cutting edge of offering plug-in features that connect to other companies, such as Facebook.

MailChimp may not offer the flashiest email templates, but their online email creator is fairly easy to use. They also provide merge tags, autoresponders, segmenting contacts into groups, and simple performance tracking tools. Those terms may sound like Greek to you, but they are nice features to use as you get more experienced. MailChimp also allows you to set up delivery times based on your subscribers' time zones. That way, everyone receives your email at the same specific hour of the day no matter where they live.

The one downside to MailChimp is their lack of telephone support. If you prefer talking to a human being when dealing with technical issues, you might consider another service. Otherwise, you can receive support by email, live chat, and a large knowledgebase with how-to articles, videos, and tutorials.

MailChimp currently offers a "Forever Free" plan, which allows authors to send 12,000 emails for up to 2,000 subscribers per month (or 6 emails per month to 2,000 subscribers). Their monthly paid plans are usually a few dollars cheaper than their competitors. Since they offer a free plan and lower monthly rates, MailChimp can be a good choice if you're just starting out with email marketing. For more information, visit: http://www.MailChimp.com

Constant Contact

Constant Contact is one of the largest email marketing services in the world. I find that their system is also the easiest to use and the most beginner-friendly option.

You can choose from a wide range of nice-looking templates to create professional-looking emails. In addition, Constant Contact makes it easy to manage your email lists and segment your subscribers if needed. Their service provides good tracking and reporting features, a built-in social media sharing tool, a free library of images to use, and one gigabyte of storage to upload your own files.

My favorite part about Constant Contact is their telephone support with a real human being. If you are technologically-challenged, talking to someone on the phone can be a life-saver. Plus, you can also get help via live chat, email, video tutorials, and a vast library of resources.

Constant Contact also offers online training and live seminars in numerous locations. These opportunities can help new authors get up to speed fast and feel like an email wizard. Their pricing tends to be a little more expensive than other competitors. However, Constant Contact offers a 60-day free trial with no credit card needed so you can test their service before deciding to buy. For more information, visit: http://www.ConstantContact.com

ConvertKit

ConvertKit is the most robust email service provider available for serious marketers. They specialize in helping you grow your list more than the other competitors mentioned. Their system is used by bestselling authors and indie writers around the world.

ConvertKit allows you to offer people your content magnets with built-in email signup forms. Their service also comes with easy to manage auto-responders allowing you to set up an email welcome sequence for new subscribers. Also, you can segment your email contacts into people who have already purchased something from you. Their customer service includes email-based support and a large knowledgebase with insightful learning material.

Pricing for ConvertKit is more expensive than other options, but they do offer a 30-day refund policy. For more information, visit: http://www.ConvertKit.com

Should Authors Use a Single or Double Opt-In Email Policy?

When you invite someone to join your email list, most email service providers will let you choose between a "single opt-in" method or a "double opt-in" method. Both methods are easy ways to gather new email subscribers. But, you many wonder what's the difference and does one option outperform the other?

The "single opt-in" method means a person fills out your signup form, hits the submit button, and has their email address instantly saved to your list. It's a single-step process that is the fastest approach for adding new subscribers.

The "double opt-in" method includes everything in the single opt-in method but adds an extra step. After someone submits their email address, a confirmation email is sent to their inbox. People must then open the confirmation email and click on a link to verify joining your list. Their email address won't be added to your list until they complete this additional step to confirm their decision.

The double opt-in method provides the advantage of knowing that every email address for each new subscriber is connected to a valid, monitored inbox. With the single opt-in method, it's easier for people to supply a fake email address and falsify joining your list. You may notice this problem if your list grows fast but your email open rates are below average.

On the other hand, the double opt-in method slows down

the sign-up process and can prevent many new subscribers from actually joining your list. People may forget to open the confirmation email and click on the required link. In addition, some people can feel frustrated by taking extra steps to join your list and receive your free content magnet.

For example, I tested the difference between single and double opt-in for one of my author clients over a two-week period. When using the double opt-in method, the statistics revealed that 38% fewer subscribers were added to the author's list. That's because they didn't respond to the confirmation email. We checked to make sure people were providing legitimate email addresses. The problem was that many people weren't following through to open the confirmation email. A 38% loss of new subscribers is a big penalty to pay just for adding a second step.

That's why I recommend the single opt-in method to build your email list. You will grow your list a lot faster if you keep the sign-up procedure quick and easy. Adding a second step causes a lot of people to neglect finishing the process. In addition, the single opt-in method is easier for people to complete using a mobile device, such as a smartphone or tablet.

There are rare cases when the double opt-in process might be a better choice. For instance, if your email campaigns suffer from very low open rates, such as 1% – 10%, then you might be getting a lot of fake email addresses from new subscribers. Switching to the double opt-in method can help diminish that problem and boost email open rates.

Also, if you decide to buy Facebook ads or Google Adwords to build your email list, a double opt-in approach can help verify that each new subscriber is a legitimate person interested in your material. For example, you might use a double opt-in method for Facebook ads to prevent people from giving you a fake email address. Meanwhile, you can use the single opt-in method for the email sign-up forms on your author website.

You can always swap between the single or double opt-in methods. Start with the single opt-in process, then make a change if you encounter the issues described above.

Email Legal Issues and Privacy Concerns

These days, it's impossible to talk about email marketing without discussing legal and privacy issues. Spamming and fraudulent activity reached a point where new laws have been created with harsh penalties in place. If you want someone to give you their email address, there are legal aspects that you must now respect.

To be clear, I'm not a lawyer and unable to render legal advice. However, the topic is important enough for you to take the appropriate measures. New regulations are constantly changing, so talk with an attorney if you have specific questions. But, let's cover a brief overview to address the acceptable policies and illegal behavior that can affect authors.

In 2018, a new European Union law went into effect called the "General Data Protection Regulation" (GDPR). This new law was designed to protect the personal data of European citizens from being harvested online and used unethically.

According to the European Commission, "Personal data is any information relating to an individual's private, professional, or public life. It can be anything from a name, a home address, a photo, an email address, bank details, posts on social networking websites, medical information, or a computer's IP address."

This new regulation is meant to curb the way companies gather and use data from people who visit their websites. However, since many American companies do business in Europe, this new law has direct consequences in the United States. In fact, Facebook and Google were hit with over $8 billion in European lawsuits two days after GDPR went into effect. Only time will tell the overall outcome. But, the state of California has already proposed new laws that will affect everyone in America.

As an author, how does GDPR apply to you? If you conduct transactions with anyone in Europe, such as readers and book buyers, you need to comply with the new laws. You can build your email list, but you must do it in a way that complies with GDPR.

Here's a breakdown of GDPR's effect in layman's terms. Building an email list is perfectly legal and fine. However, there are proper and improper ways to add people to your list. Here are some examples of the differences:

Proper ways to build your email list:

- Ask people to specifically join your email newsletter
- Offer free giveaways as an incentive to specifically join your email newsletter
- Make it clear people can unsubscribe from your email list at any time
- Only send emails related to the reason people signed up in the first place, such as receiving your e-newsletter, new book release details, and updates
- Provide a written privacy policy that details how you treat personal data with care

Improper ways to build your email list:

- Adding people to your email list without their consent
- Asking people to join your email list without explaining what you'll send in the future
- Buying an email list from a third-party without having those people's consent
- Sending unrelated emails that people didn't want or expect to receive
- Not allowing people to unsubscribe from your list whenever they want
- Failing to display a privacy policy or selling your email list to a third-party

As you can see, there's a big difference between properly

and improperly adding people to your list. When you do it legally, people can join your list with their consent and understand what they will receive in the future. You make everything clear up-front and avoid being unethical.

In contrast, you can fail to comply with GDPR by adding someone to your email list without their consent, making it difficult for people to unsubscribe, or failing to explain the types of emails that they'll receive from you in the future.

Here's the bottom line: Don't be a jerk.

Don't add people to your list without their consent. Don't send emails that only promote your stuff and lack real value for the reader. Don't make it hard for people to unsubscribe. Instead, respect people's privacy, respect their expectations, and respect their decision to leave if they choose.

If you need help creating a privacy policy for your website, consult with an attorney, your webmaster, or copy the text from another author's website whom you know has the correct language in place. You can also Google "privacy policy generator" to find free and inexpensive options for assistance.

GDPR occurred because too many marketers and too many companies were being jerks. They felt entitled to gather people's personal online data and do whatever they wanted. I'm grateful the EU decided to do something about this worldwide problem. Now that you're aware of GDPR, take steps to comply with new law on your author website and protect people's personal data. Sometimes, the best way to improve your marketing is to treat customers with the respect they deserve.

What Is a Typical Email Open Rate?

When you send an email to the subscribers on your list, how many people will open it and read the contents? How do you know if your emails are effective or under-performing? The most common way to measure the performance of an email you send is called the "open rate." To explain this term clearly, I pulled information provided by MailChimp, which is one of the most popular email service providers among authors.

According to MailChimp, the "open rate" is a percentage number that tells you how many email subscribers successfully opened your email campaign. To determine this number, MailChimp loads a tiny, transparent image into each email that is sent, and then counts how often that image is downloaded among the delivered emails. The image is invisible to your subscribers and only used to gather the "open rate" data.

Every month, MailChimp scans billions of emails sent by millions of their customers to track the average level of response. According to a report they released in March, 2018, the average open rate for all emails across the board was 20.8%. However, their report also included data for separate categories, such as Media and Publishing. Authors fall into the Media and Publishing category, and the average open rate for that group was 21.9%. In other words, you should typically expect around 20% - 22% of your email subscribers to open the emails that you send.

However, I have several author clients who consistently receive 25% – 30% open rates with their email campaigns. Success is based on several factors, such as how often you send emails and how interesting your audience finds the content within your emails. But, you can use an industry average of 20% to know if you are outperforming or lagging behind your peers.

Now, you might feel like a 20% open rate is a low number. What about the other 80%? Why is email considered effective if only 2 out of every 10 people see what you send? Consider the alternatives, such as social media or direct mail.

As I described in the beginning of this book, Facebook only lets 5% – 15% of your fans see a post that you place on their platform for free. If you want the other 85% – 95% of your fans to see your post, you must pay Facebook money by buying "boosted posts" or "sponsored posts." That additional expense adds up fast. Plus, Twitter and the other social media platforms provide even less response than Facebook.

Direct mail is another alternative. However, it is expensive, time-consuming, and requires getting people's mailing address. What would you rather do? Send people a quick email with links to easily buy your book, or send letters in the mail hoping people don't throw your offer into the trash? You get my point. Email is a superior option. Plus, most people aren't too excited about giving authors their home mailing address.

Keep in mind that an open rate of 20% doesn't mean only 20% of your email subscribers will hear about your book. Since you're able to send more than one email to your list, different people will choose to open your different emails. Some people who open Email A may not open Email B and vice versa. By sending several emails over time, you're able to connect with a larger percentage of your email list than just 20%. In my personal opinion, your total reach could be as high as 30% – 40% over multiple email campaigns. That's why email is considered one of the most cost-effective ways to market a book.

Help...My Email List Isn't Growing!

What do you do when your email list grows at a snail's pace? Have you ever felt like your list seems stuck at the same number for weeks? Sometimes, it seems that unsubscribes may outweigh the new subscribers. Maybe you're experiencing frustration about the lack of new subscribers, which is why you're reading this book.

Believe me, I know how you feel. A lot of the recommendations I'm giving you were born out of my own frustration. For several years, I didn't give my email list the attention and priority that it deserved. I didn't offer any incentives. I buried my email newsletter signup box at the bottom of my website.

Meanwhile, I began to wonder if email was a waste time

that I should abandon altogether. Fortunately, I didn't throw the baby out with bath water. I realized that email wasn't the problem. I was the problem. I was the reason my email list wasn't growing. But, the good news was that if I was the reason for the problem, then I could also be the one to implement a solution.

Sometimes, the best solutions are the simplest. In my case, the lack of growth was simply a lack of focus. I wasn't practicing what I preached to my own clients. I was too busy consulting, teaching other authors, and neglecting the work required to make progress. So, I decided to get serious.

I took the exact strategies laid out in this book and applied them to myself. I spent 30 days creating the content magnets and landing pages to get my house in order. Guess what? Within another 30 days, I quickly tripled my average signup rate compared to the previous doldrums. On a daily basis, I started to receive 3 – 4 times more new subscribers than before. So, I know that these techniques work. Plus, they work for my author clients, regardless of experience or genre.

If you find yourself stymied by a lack of new subscribers, I feel your pain. But, that pain doesn't have to linger. You have the control to improve your list growth, and you must take the necessary action.

Assuming your expectations are realistic, a lack of list growth could be related to one of the following issues:

1. You are too stingy with your content

If you want a lot of people to join your email list, then you must give them a compelling reason to sign up. People don't share their email addresses lightly. They've already got enough junk mail in their inbox. Therefore, a lack of response could be a direct reflection to your lack of generosity.

For example, if you only offer people a sample chapter or a short article as your content magnet, they will regard you as stingy. Most people know that authors have more content to give away than just a brief excerpt. Thus, the fastest way to attract more email subscribers is to boost your generosity. If you write fiction, give away a substantial short story. Or, if you have a series of several related books, give away the entire first novel in the series. People will be excited to see they can get a whole book for free.

If you write non-fiction, offer a free video teaching series. Or, package several articles together into a set. Give away multiple e-books at the same time. For instance, when I started giving away three free e-books on my website, my email signup rate dramatically increased. Three is more generous than one. Don't be a scrooge. Boost your generosity and make your content magnet an offer that people can't refuse.

2. Your content magnet titles are boring

Besides a lack of generosity, another big deterrent to email signups is a lack of attention-grabbing titles. I mentioned this principle in Chapter 2. Never forget that people cannot see the free content you're offering until after they join your email list. They are taking a leap of faith based primarily on the title of your content magnet. If your title is boring, many people will not respond.

If your list growth is stagnant, be honest with yourself and examine if you created boring titles for your content magnets. Don't ride a dead horse. Create better titles and you will see a better response. For instance, you wouldn't be reading this book if I had titled it, *A Study of Author Email Activities*. Titles matter. You get my point.

3. Your artwork or landing page looks homemade

If you want skeptical people to take you seriously, you need to look professional. First impressions matter. If the graphics or cover art for your content magnet look home-made, don't get upset by a lackluster response. If the layout and marketing copy on your email signup landing page is mundane, don't blame other people. It's your fault.

Growing your email list is too important to treat haphaz-ardly. Hire a graphic designer or rework your cover art and landing page until it sizzles. If you need ideas, look at the images, cover art, and landing pages for authors who are highly successful in your genre. Mimic elements of their success to help you appear more professional. You have complete control over your online appearance.

4. Your audience reach is too small

You might be incredibly generous, look professional, and offer content magnets with clever titles, but still experience slow list growth. In this case, the problem is usually related to a lack of audience reach. Put simply, there aren't enough people seeing your amazing offer. You can overcome the issue in several ways.

If possible, partner with other authors or organizations who are willing to promote your content magnet to their audience. For instance, it's common for novelists to band together, each contribute a short story, and compile those stories into an exclusive anthology. Then, the anthology is promoted by every author to his or her own audience. But, it also gives all of the authors access to multiple new audiences. Everyone wins by sharing in the increased exposure together.

You can also foster relationships with organizations who already have massive website traffic. For example, one of my author clients developed a connection with the editor at PsychologyToday.com to write guest blog posts whenever she desires. *Psychology Today* receives thousands of visitors to their website every week. At the end of each blog post, my client includes a promotion and a link to her free content magnet in her author bio paragraph. When readers of her blog posts see the free offer, they can easily click on the link and join her author email list. She gets new email subscribers by converting traffic from another large website for free.

If you don't have partnerships available like I described above, you can always buy targeted Facebook ads to get more eyeballs on your free content magnet. I have clients who routinely add over 100 new email subscribers per month spending $500 or less on Facebook ads.

Remember the frustration about my email list that I

described at the beginning of this section? Like me, you may feel frustrated if your list isn't growing according to expectations. But, like me, you also have control over the situation. I want you to succeed and reach your goals. The answers may not be easy, but they do work. If your email list is stagnant, use the suggestions above to get out of a funk and get your list growing again.

The Big Question

Besides dealing with concerns about list growth, legal issues, choosing a service provider, and typical open rates, there is one concern that plagues authors about email marketing more than anything else:

> *Once I get people to give me their email address, how do I turn those subscribers into book sales?*

Obviously, the purpose of building a list isn't to give away free material and hoard email addresses. The purpose is to generate consistent book sales. You may even have high open rates but low book sales. Just because people open your emails doesn't mean they'll automatically buy your products. The good news is that email offers more than one way to create the sales you desire.

Email is quite versatile. There are multiple ways to turn subscribers into book buyers. Each method is so beneficial that we'll look at the details in separate chapters, which I'll cover next:

- Chapter 5 - How to create an automated email onboard sequence
- Chapter 6 - How to send persuasive sales emails
- Chapter 7 - How to deliver effective email newsletters

CREATE AN EMAIL ONBOARD SEQUENCE

Imagine you're having a nice conversation with a friend named Pam when another friend named Steve walks up and says, "Hey guys, what are you talking about?" You want to include Steve in the conversation, so you quickly recap what you were discussing with Pam to catch Steve up to speed. After Steve hears your recap, he can participate with you and Pam going forward. He's now a "part of the conversation."

But, what if you didn't give Steve the courtesy of a recap? How would he feel? Imagine if Steve walked up and said, "Hey guys, what are you talking about?" Yet, this time, you ignored him or forced him to figure out the discussion on his own? From Steve's point of view, he would probably feel confused. He may even get frustrated, decide to leave your conversation, and never talk to you again.

When people join your email list, they are joining a conversation already taking place between you and your fans. New email subscribers are like Steve in the example above. Most people are not familiar with you, your books, or the content that you write. They are entering a discussion that is unfamiliar, and they can feel like the odd man out. If you want new people to buy your books, you can use email to give them a "quick recap" and catch them up to speed.

I call this process an "email onboard sequence," which is just a fancy term for sending a sequence of emails that inform new people about you and your books. This brilliant strategy came to my attention from *USA Today* bestselling indie novelist, Mark Dawson (https://markjdawson.com). Mark writes suspense-packed spy thriller stories, and his books have been downloaded over two million times. One reason for Mark's outstanding success is that he doesn't take new email subscribers for granted. He never assumes people are familiar with his novels. Nor does he assume people are immediately ready to buy his books.

Instead, Mark believes that his new email subscribers need to be "caught up to speed." They need a quick recap about his books before they become buyers. For example, Mark has 15 novels that are all part of the same spy thriller fiction series. When people join his email list, he sends an automated series of nine emails over a 30-day period that gives new subscribers samples from several of his novels. It's a very generous strategy that would lead some authors to think he is giving away the farm for free.

In addition, you might think new subscribers would be

turned off by receiving a lot of emails from Mark within the first month. Yet, the opposite reaction occurs. Not only do subscribers stay on his list, they buy a lot of his books. That's because Mark's email onboard sequence helps people engage on a much deeper level with his books. In essence, he weeds out "the wheat from the chaff" by identifying his serial readers as fast as possible. Those serial readers go on to buy multiple books from his series and drive a lot of sales. Email provides an automated way to identify and nurture your serial readers.

Don't Take New Email Subscribers for Granted

When someone joins your email list, do you expect them to figure out everything about your books on their own? Are you hoping they'll immediately buy books after downloading your free content magnet? Those are unrealistic expectations. How many times have you bought something after only one sample? Most people tend to buy new products until after they've developed a comfort level with the item.

Thus, if you don't help develop a comfort level with new email subscribers, it can explain why they may join your list but never buy your books. They feel out of the loop. Worse, they might feel like you took them for granted. When someone feels that way, they'll tend to ignore the emails you send in the future or unsubscribe from your list altogether.

How do you bring new subscribers up to speed and make them feel appreciated?

Create an email onboard sequence

"Onboarding" means familiarizing new people with your products and services. Email enables you to onboard new subscribers by setting up a series of autoresponders. An "autoresponder" is an email that you create and schedule ahead of time that can be automatically sent to every new subscriber as they join your list. You can create a sequence of these automated emails that work in unison to bring new subscribers up to speed. I'll show you a few samples of sequences later in this chapter. The benefit of an automated sequence is that once you create the system, it will run in the background 24/7 every day of the year.

If you've never heard the terms "onboarding" or "autoresponders," you could be going into technology shock right now. I understand if you're thinking, "Really, Rob?! Your first recommendation about email is to set up a sophisticated email sequence? That's too complex for my experience level." Believe me, I sympathize with that perspective.

If you're a first-time author or someone who isn't comfortable with technology, the idea of an email onboard sequence may seem overwhelming. But, here's the reason why I'm recommending this technique before explaining simpler methods, such as sales emails and newsletters:

If you don't bring new email subscribers "up to speed" in the beginning, the response to sales emails and newsletters that you send in the future could be diminished.

Is it optional to create an email onboard sequence? Yes. You do not have to take this step. To be honest, most authors don't do it, because no one told them it was possible.

However, I'm encouraging you to consider an onboard sequence, because it's one of the most effective methods to welcome new subscribers, identify highly-coveted serial readers, and make people feel more comfortable buying your books. If you're still with me, let me explain how the process works.

An email onboard sequence is determined by your genre and how many books you've written. The purpose of these emails is to explain who you are, provide additional samples from your books, and get people more familiar with your material.

For instance, if you've only written one book, then sending 1 – 3 automated emails to welcome new subscribers may be sufficient. In contrast, if you've written several books or a series of books, then you might send 5 – 10 emails spread out over 30 – 45 days. Each email in the sequence is strategically sent to share extra samples that make people feel appreciated. The faster that new subscribers become familiar with you and your books, the faster they'll feel comfortable purchasing.

I also recommend concluding an onboard email sequence with a short survey that helps you learn more about your subscribers' demographics and their buying preferences.

Here's the principle that explains why an automated onboard sequence is effective:

The sooner you build trust with readers, the sooner you can ask for the book sale.

When most people join your email list, they're not necessarily ready to buy. They need to trust you first. By "trust," I mean that people need to believe it will be worth their money and time to read your book. The fact is that most Americans do not read books, and those who do read are picky about what they like. If you want to convert email subscribers into customers, focus on building their trust as fast as possible.

Sending automated emails with extra samples of your books allows people to get a deeper feel for your material and writing style. Also, it makes you seem like a generous, thoughtful author. By sending onboard emails with additional value, it becomes easier to ask subscribers to buy your books.

For instance, when you send the second or third email in your sequence, insert an offer to buy one of your books and provide a link to purchase. As you give more samples in the remaining emails of your sequence, include a call-to-action to purchase. Then, track how many people open your automated emails and click the links to buy. The data will tell you if the system is working.

Obviously, the samples you include in your onboard sequence need to contain quality content that would convince skeptical readers. But, that's the benefit to building an automated system. If you send new subscribers a few emails, ask for the sale, but don't get much response, then you know your samples need adjusting.

The good news is that it doesn't cost you anything to determine the flaw. Nor does it cost anything to adjust your onboard sequence with better samples and persuasive language. You can keep tweaking the system until the results improve.

Let's look at three options to create an email onboard sequence based on different author scenarios. These aren't the only options, just ideas to get you started:

Onboard Sequence for Author with a Single Book

Day 1 – Give content magnet from author website

Day 3 – Give first excerpt from book

Day 5 – Give second excerpt from book

Day 7 – Give third excerpt from book

Day 10 – Reader survey

Onboard Sequence for Author with 5 Unrelated Books

Day 1 – Give content magnet from author website

Day 3 – Give excerpt from Book 1

Day 5 – Give excerpt from Book 2

Day 7 – Give excerpt from Book 3

Day 9 – Give excerpt from Book 4

Day 11 – Give excerpt from Book 5

Day 14 – Reader survey

Onboard Sequence for Author with 5 Books in a Series

Day 1 – Give away Book 1 as content magnet

Day 3 – Give excerpt from Book 2

Day 5 – Give another excerpt from Book 2

Day 12 – Give excerpt from Book 3

Day 15 – Give excerpt from Book 4

Day 19 – Give excerpt from Book 5

Day 25 – Reader survey

These examples are meant to show you various options you can consider. You do not have to copy these email onboard sequences verbatim. Feel free to create a sequence that fits your specific needs and the number of books you have written.

Every email should include a short note from the author along with links to purchase the book. Inject your personality and a friendly tone into the email message. Your words can be brief. Remember than your goal is to bring the reader "up to speed" on what you write and why you enjoy writing.

Again, I highly recommend exuding generosity with the

length of your book excerpts. Give away an entire chapter or several related chapters within each email of your sequence. Savvy authors are willing to give away entire books for free, especially if it's the first book in a series.

For example, giving away the first book in a trilogy will help drive sales of the second and third book. You may lose money on the first book, but actually make more money in the long run by increasing sales of the second book, third book, and so forth.

You will also notice that I included a reader survey at the end of each onboard sequence. Do not neglect this step. Conducting a brief survey can provide invaluable details about your readers, such as demographics, how often they read books in your genre, purchasing preferences, other favorite authors, new topics for your next book, etc. Some email service providers, such as Constant Contact, include survey capabilities within their system. Otherwise, you can use inexpensive online options, such as SurveyMonkey (https://www.SurveyMonkey.com).

Creating an onboard sequence can be easier than you might think. If you're unfamiliar with setting up auto-responder emails, consult with the customer service team at your email service provider. Yes, it takes a little extra work. But, once your system is in place, it will run in the background and help drive book sales while you write your next book or go on vacation.

Email is an amazing tool that can be automated to help new people quickly become familiar with your books. Don't take new subscribers for granted. Onboard everyone with a well-timed sequence.

However, onboarding new subscribers with automated messages is just one way email marketing can help sell more books. In the next chapter, I'll explain how to use a more common form of email marketing, which is sending persuasive sales emails.

6

SEND PERSUASIVE SALES EMAILS

Take a look at the two statements below. Do you see any appreciable difference?

- Listen to me. This is important.
- LISTEN TO ME. **THIS IS IMPORTANT!**

Both statements contain the exact same words. You could reason that each sentence says the same thing. Yet, the second statement uses all capital letters, a bolded font, and ends with an exclamation point. Notice how the second statement is more effective at grabbing your attention and motivating you to do something, which is to listen to me.

These two sentences illustrate an important principle about email marketing:

Your email subscribers will always take their cue from you.

People will not understand that something is important unless you tell them it is important. A "cue" means a signal to act. As the author, it is your job to initiate the cue for your email recipients to take action. If executed correctly, your email subscribers will respond to your cue. For instance, if you want to sell more books, you must cue a desire to purchase in the mind of your email subscribers.

Hear me LOUD and **CLEAR**: Your email subscribers have no responsibility to buy your books. Instead, it is your responsibility to motivate email subscribers to purchase.

The first step to motivate other people is to get their attention and make your request feel important. Therefore, your subscribers always take their cue from you. Here's how this principle applies to selling books using email:

- People will not buy your new book unless you make a big deal about it.
- People will not buy your backlist books unless you renew their interest.
- People will not write Amazon reviews unless you encourage them to do it.
- People will not attend your live event or book-signing unless you remind them.
- People will never know that you hit a bestseller list unless you tell them.

Your audience always takes their cue from you. Your cue acts as a signal that it's time for your audience to take action. Without any cues, there is little action.

Email is one of the best ways to tell people that something important is happening. Within an individual email, you can send a message that incites people to make a purchase. I call this type of communication "sales emails."

Sales emails are a separate tactic from the onboard sequence described in the previous chapter. They are also different from newsletters, which I'll discuss in Chapter 7. Different email techniques apply to different situations.

For example, if you have a new book coming out, you won't sell many copies if you only mention the launch in one issue of a newsletter. One newsletter announcement isn't enough to cue people and convince them to purchase. If you want a lot of people to buy a new book, you must remind everyone to buy your new book several times.

In many cases, your audience may need to receive 4 – 7 reminders to get them off of the fence. It's not about beating people over the head into submission. Instead, you're facing the reality that most people are busy, distracted, or never see your first few messages.

For instance, if the average email open rate of an email newsletter is 20%, then 80% of the other subscribers aren't seeing your message to buy your new book. That's why certain situations call for sending specific sales emails with a clear call-to-action, such as "Buy my new book," "Attend my live event," "Purchase my backlist book," etc.

Just to be clear, sales emails are meant to be interspersed and peppered around your newsletters. You wouldn't send a sales email and a newsletter on the same day. Just send your newsletter. But, there can be a lot of time in between news-letter issues, so sending separate sales emails helps fill-in the gaps during a book launch, major event, or important product campaign. Or, if you decide not to do a newsletter, then sales emails will be the primary way to communicate with your audience. If the frequency of emails gives you cause for concern, remember this point:

You can never over-communicate with your email subscribers if you send them emails with interesting information.

When you let people know that your new book is available, that announcement qualifies as interesting information. Inviting people to meet you in-person counts as interesting information. Reminding people that a backlist book offers relevant value also qualifies as interesting information.

Plus, if you combine interesting information with limited-time price discounts, early-bird savings, exclusive bonuses, or other incentives, then your sales email definitely qualifies as interesting information.

Let's be honest. Will some people view a sales email as being too promotional and unsubscribe from your email list? Absolutely. Let them go. Good riddance. You don't want your email list to be filled with moochers who never buy anything. You can't survive as an author unless you generate revenue.

Never forget that you've been the generous person in the email relationship from the very beginning. You gave away free content magnets when people joined your email list.

So, ignore people who complain your emails are too promotional. In reality, their attitude reflects a selfish perspective. Disregard their comments, keep your author self-esteem strong, and hold your marketing head high.

Okay, that last paragraph may have drifted into a personal counseling session. But, never let the fear of offending email subscribers keep you from promoting your books. Your audience takes their cue from you. People will not purchase unless you remind and motivate them to purchase.

Just in case you're one of the rare authors who believes marketing is unnecessary or that books sell by word of mouth alone, I have two questions:

1. Why are you reading this book about marketing? (gotcha)

2. How many more books could you have sold in the past if you employed wise marketing principles?

You may be satisfied with your past sales. But, I would argue that you could have sold twice as many books if had employed wise marketing principles from the beginning. Why make that mistake going forward? I'd like to see you reach the full potential of your book sales. As my poker-playing uncle used to say, "There is never a good reason to leave money on the table."

Your email list provides the best way to build trust with people and transform them into happy buyers. But, they will not become happy buyers if they rarely hear about your books or receive infrequent communication. Use individual sales emails to make sure people know when it's time to act.

Enough with the theoretical discussion. Let's examine common marketing situations almost every author may encounter where sales emails can be useful:

- Sales emails for a book launch
- Sales emails for author events
- Sales emails for backlist books

Sales Emails for a Book Launch

Some authors joke that launching a new book feels like birthing a new baby – just with less pain. However, if you've had kids, think about the excitement you felt when your child was born. You wanted to tell the world. You sent people happy pictures. You mailed announcement cards. You posted exuberant messages on Facebook. Expressing joy is normal behavior for new parents, and most people are happy to share the enthusiasm.

Likewise, how excited do you feel when you "birth" a new book? You put your heart and soul into writing the manuscript. When it's ready for the world to see, do you minimize your enthusiasm? No, you should express your joy just like a happy new parent. Convey that joy to your email list. If your joy is authentic, many subscribers will share your excitement and buy a book.

However, remember that most people on your email list are busy, distracted, and flooded with advertising to buy stuff. Therefore, you can't just say, "Buy my book!" one time and expect people to drop what they're doing. Share your joy multiple times to make sure people know it's time to buy a copy of your "new baby."

During your book launch window, you need to send several sales emails if you hope to get a significant response. There is no hard and fast rule to follow. Every launch is unique based on the author and the genre. However, you can segment book launch sales emails into these three periods: *Pre-launch, Launch, and Post-launch*

In the pre-launch period, your goal is to generate a sense of curiosity and anticipation from your email subscribers. Okay, you're thinking, "Rob, tell me something I don't know." Well, here's what you may not know. There are specific ways to send emails that build anticipation. Use these three options during your pre-launch book phase:

Pre-Launch Sales Email #1 – Cover Reveal

Months before your new book arrives, send an announcement to your email list when you finalize the cover art. Send a picture of the cover and share your excitement. However, in order to prevent seeming narcissistic, include a sample chapter or substantial excerpt from your book to whet people's appetite for your content. Promote the book, not just the cover. If you want to be clever, tell subscribers that you are "leaking" exclusive material only for them to see.

Pre-Launch Sales Email #2 – Content Sneak Peek

As time gets closer to your book launch, make a full sample chapter or substantial excerpt available. Don't be stingy. Share the best parts of your book, not just the first chapter.

For example, Hollywood studios always shows the best parts of a movie in the television commercial. That technique is by design because it works. Copy the same approach. Send a sales email to your list giving everyone a "sneak peek" at your best material. Encourage subscribers to reply with their favorite quotes from the content that you have given them. Based on the time period leading up to launch, you could send 2 – 4 sales emails that offer featured content excerpts.

Pre-Launch Sales Email #3 – Promote Pre-orders

This step is optional based on if you decide to run a pre-order campaign for a new book. If so, start promoting your purchase incentives 4 – 8 weeks before the book launch. If you're new to the idea of a pre-order campaign, let me explain. Before your new book can be shipped to readers, it will be available to purchase at most retailers several weeks before the official launch date. People who pre-order early will have to wait to receive the book. But, readers pre-order to be first in line to receive and enjoy an author's book before anyone else.

Traditional publishers love pre-order campaigns, because a rush of early sales creates leverage to boost retail bookstore orders and help propel books onto the major bestseller lists.

Many authors entice readers to pre-order books by offering exclusive incentives, such as bonus content, deep price discounts, prizes, accompanying workbooks, access to meet the author, etc. However, you must announce these incentives once they're available, then remind people when the pre-order window is about to close.

Sales emails that focus on promoting pre-orders and reminding people that incentives will disappear engage the power of FOMO, which means the "Fear Of Missing Out." When people realize that a good thing is about to disappear, a sense of urgency will encourage them to take action.

Wise authors send several sales emails during the pre-order phase to motivate their subscribers to buy early. The message can be a simple reminder to be the first in line or capitalize on exclusive incentives. But, people won't respond if you remind them about the pre-order opportunity.

As you shift from the pre-launch phase to actual book launch period, there are different types of sales emails you can create. Here are some options for sales emails you can send when your book is officially released:

Launch Day Sales Email

The first day your book is available to purchase at the major retailers, send a sales email to your entire list announcing the big news. Briefly explain why you wrote the book and the benefits readers will receive from buying a copy. If there are any special discounts offered during your launch, mention the opportunity to save money. Always provide links to multiple retailers to avoid playing favorites. Entice your email subscribers to open your launch day email with a spicy subject line that sums up your book in one sentence, such as:

Fiction subject line examples:

- A sleepy Kentucky town. A murdered sheriff. A whodunit you cannot put down.
- A sarcastic guy. A snarky girl. Whose heart will fall in love first?
- My new book is here! Get it before anyone else.

Non-fiction subject line examples:

- An insider's look at America's first president
- A shocking story of kids growing up with homeless parents
- Discover why email is an author's ticket to the bestseller lists

Post-Launch Sales Email

After your new book has been officially launched, don't feel embarrassed to continue promoting it. If you stop now, you can lose a lot of sales momentum and word of mouth. Keep up the excitement with post-launch sales emails. Remember, your book is your baby, and new parents don't stop celebrating a birth after just one week.

Send two or three follow-up sales emails within 30 days after your launch to remind subscribers that your new book is available. Besides including more content excerpts or highlighting a price discount, here are two other ways to differentiate a sales email during the post-launch period:

Social Influence Sales Email

One of the most persuasive ways to get email subscribers to buy your book is to let other people sing its praises. This marketing technique is called "social influence." You use positive comments from a respected peer to influence other people's behavior. For instance, you can send a sales email to your list that features a testimonial about your book from a well-known leader, musician, athlete, pastor, executive, doctor, actor, etc. If you don't have a high-profile testimonial, insert several 5-star reviews from Amazon to show social proof that people are enjoying your book.

In other situations, your book might have received a mention from a national or regional magazine, industry journal, popular blogger, or YouTube personality. If someone praises your book, don't keep the kudos to yourself. Tout the testimonial by sending a sales email to your list. Use positive comments from other people as social influence to motivate your subscribers to purchase.

Bestseller or Award Sales Email

Shortly after your new book launch, there might be occasions when exciting or unexpected news occur. You might hit a bestsellers list. You might receive a major industry review. You might surpass a sales milestone within the first 30 – 90 days. Whenever something positive happens to your book, even months down the road, send a sales email to spread the good news.

Include your email subscribers in the excitement by explaining how they helped make your success possible. Share your accomplishments with them because launching a book is always a team sport. When your fans hear that your book is doing well, it gives them more confidence to share word of mouth, which is essential to growing sales.

Just like proud parents, you should be proud of your new book. Share the joy with your subscribers throughout the pre-launch, launch, and post-launch phases.

Sales Emails for Author Events

There is much more to an author's life than just launching a new book. There are champagne lunches with Hollywood agents, whirlwind book tours on private jets, sold-out book signings with adoring fans. Okay, maybe not. Authors can always dream, right? You may not be treated like James Patterson or J.K. Rowling, but exciting events can happen to any author.

For example, you might get an appearance on national radio or television, interviewed on a popular podcast, go on a book signing tour, hit the speaking circuit, etc. Wring extra value out of those situations by sending email reminders to your list about those author events. Your subscribers cannot participate if they don't know an upcoming event exists.

One of my former clients is Hollywood producer and *New York Times* bestselling author, DeVon Franklin. DeVon frequently appears on national media, such as *Good Morning America* and *The Breakfast Club*. A day or two before an upcoming interview, he sends an email announcement to all of his subscribers. The morning of the interview, he sends a brief reminder email. Afterwards, if DeVon receives a link to the video or audio footage from the interview, he sends a follow-up email for everyone to watch. This is a great example of keeping your email list in the loop on your major activities.

As people see you discuss your book in the media or in-person, you will reap additional sales and word of mouth. Your email list can be a powerful force to drive extra buzz around your public appearances. However, if you don't keep subscribers informed, they can't join the party.

Sales Emails for Backlist Books

Every author wants their new book to keep selling for years and their old books to maintain a long life. However, the antiquated publishing industry gives most books an extremely short window to be considered "new." After being in print for just a few months. new books soon become classified as a "backlist book."

The term "backlist" means that a new book no longer receives primary attention and resources from the publishing house. The book must survive on its own. It's like putting an old horse out to pasture and seeing how long it can live. But, you don't have to let your books endure such a depressing fate.

Use sale emails to revive interest in your backlist books. Ironically, the key to selling older books is to use same approach you employed to promote your new book:

You must convince yourself that your "old" book is still "new."

Think about it. When someone first hears about a book - no matter how old - it's still a new book to them. Books don't have an expiration date like a spoiled carton of milk. Books can remain wildly popular even decades after they've been published.

I proved this concept when I helped the backlist book, *Boundaries*, become a *New York Times* bestseller after being in print for over 23 years. The book enjoyed consistent sales, but never hit the world's top bestseller list. That's because the book didn't receive the constant attention it deserved.

One of the ways I boosted interest in this "old" book was to build a large email list and send frequent updates with content samples. Even though the content was written two decades prior, people still found *Boundaries* relevant to their lives. As more people became aware of the "old" book, sales increased and *Boundaries* hit the *New York Times* bestseller list for several months in a row.

No matter how old your book might be, you can still sell more copies if the content is professional and relevant to the public. You might need to update the cover art to look modern. But, people don't buy books based on the publication date. They buy books based on an enjoyable reading experience.

Send sales emails to your subscribers that remind them how your "old" books are still relevant. There are a variety of ways to renew interest, such as:

1. Send a sales email with a limited-time price discount and free samples.

2. Send a sales email that highlights a new endorsement or the amount of 5-star reviews on Amazon.

3. Send a sales email with exclusive incentives to buy a back-list book, such as bonus content, a short story, a free workbook, or win a private phone call with author.

In short, there's no such thing as an "old" book. Your book is only old if you act like it's old. Treat all of your books like they are new, and your email subscribers will respond likewise. Use sales emails to remind them of your book's value.

If you doggedly believe that books should only be judged as old or new, then feel free to buy me a 20-year old "worthless" Ferrari. I'd be happy to drive it.

Rules to Remember for Sales Emails

Whenever you send sales emails to your subscribers, below are some rules to follow that will help maximize the response rate:

1. Always display a persuasive subject line that entices people to open your email.

2. Always put the most important item or call to action at the top of the email.

3. Always display easy-to-see links for people to buy or pre-order your book.

4. Always include purchase links to multiple retailers. Don't only show Amazon, because not everyone buys from them and other retailers deserve some attention as well.

5. Always provide text-based hyperlinks to purchase your

book, because image links won't appear on some email services. Thus, people can't see how to buy your book.

6. Always ask your email subscribers to share and forward your email to their friends.

To recap, say this final rule out loud...

Your email subscribers always take their cue from you.

If you act like your book is no big deal, then no one will think buying your book is a big deal. You must make the effort to stand out in people's mind. Will every email you send generate a big response? No. That's why frequency of communication is an essential part of creating sales. By sending sales emails, you can wield greater influence over your subscribers and motivate them to take action.

Do You View Your Subscribers as Fans?

As described in the previous section, your email subscribers take their cue from the frequency of your emails. However, they also take their cue from the tone of your email language. By "tone," I mean the way you talk to your subscribers and the text you display in the body of your emails. For example, which question below most resembles the attitude you feel about your email list:

Do you view your email subscribers as fans who like you?

Or, do you view your email subscribers as moochers who just want everything from you for free?

The way you answer this question makes a big difference. If you believe your subscribers are your fans, then you will act and write in a positive manner. First, you won't be afraid to send emails, because you believe your subscribers like you and want you to succeed. It's much easier to communicate with people whom you feel are your supporters. We like to talk to people who also like us.

Plus, if you believe your subscribers are your fans, then the language within your emails will sound more positive and confident. Your sales emails will convey an upbeat attitude based on genuine enthusiasm that rubs off on the reader. People like to receive email messages from authors who are encouraging and confident, rather than downbeat, meek, or frustrated.

In contrast, if you fear your email subscribers or view them as freeloaders, your negative attitude will undermine the tone of your email campaigns. As a result, creating new sales emails will feel like a waste of time. Worse, your ability to persuade subscribers into buying books will be diminished.

Let's say one of your email sales campaigns doesn't go well and people buy fewer books than you hoped. Don't lose enthusiasm for your subscribers. If your enthusiasm wanes, your audience will sense the change and adopt the negative cue that you exude. It's okay to feel disappointed if your subscribers don't respond as expected. But, keep that disappointment to yourself and maintain positive cues with your email language.

In the digital world, your email subscribers are the closest thing to your true fans. Treat them like valuable followers. Enjoy talking to them. Respond to their comments that you receive. Send emails that cue their interest. As you share your genuine excitement, the level of response will usually increase.

Let's be realistic. Will it take a long time for some email subscribers to eventually purchase? Yes. Will some people never purchase anything? Yes. Will some people unsubscribe and drop off your list? Sure, but those issues are normal for every author. When you know how to grow your list with enticing content magnets, you can quickly replace anyone who leaves.

Your audience always takes their cue from you. Don't be afraid to send sales emails and maintain an enthusiastic tone with fans. Your subscribers want to see you succeed. This principle also applies to sending potent email newsletters, which I'll explain in the next chapter.

7

STAY IN TOUCH WITH EMAIL NEWSLETTERS

Before we move forward, let's conduct a quick recap. In Chapter 5, I explained how to create an "email onboard sequence" that welcomes new subscribers. That sequence typically runs for 14 – 30 days. In Chapter 6, I discussed how to send various types of "sales emails." These emails are typically sent around a new book launch, which may run for 30 – 90 days. But, these short time windows beg an important question:

How do you stay in touch with your email subscribers over the long-term?

Once people complete your email onboard sequence, what happens next? After you finish a book launch, what comes afterwards? Do you disappear until your next book launch? What if your next book is a year or more away?

Be wary of viewing email as only a promotional tool to send

promotional campaigns during a book launch and then go AWOL. Here's the challenge you face with that short-sighted approach:

If you don't actively stay in the minds of your readers, you risk your readers forgetting that you exist.

Regardless if you write fiction or non-fiction, there are at least 1,000 other authors trying to get your email subscribers to read their books instead of yours. You can be sure they are marketing to your fans and attempting to woo their interest away from you.

If you want to risk losing your fans by neglecting to communicate with them, that is your decision to make. You will have to bear the consequences. In my experience, there are very few situations where you can ignore your audience and get away with it. Here are some rare exceptions:

1. If you are lucky enough to write a breakout novel, an irresistible memoir, or a revolutionary non-fiction book that makes you a household name, then you can get away with ignoring your audience.

2. If you are a perennial bestseller who knows your publisher will do everything for you because your books pay their bills, then you can get away with ignoring your audience.

3. If you are filthy rich and can bankroll a national advertising campaign with your own money, then you can get away with ignoring your audience.

4. If you are a former president of the United States and got a book deal after running the free world, then you can get away with ignoring your audience.

If you do not fall into the categories listed above, then you cannot get away with ignoring your audience. Welcome to the humble life of a typical author. But, life can be equally satisfying if you nurture the readers who love your books. But, many authors feel a sense of hesitancy about nurturing their readers via email based on two fears:

- What if I risk offending my email subscribers and they leave my list?
- I don't know how to send effective emails to fans. What if I do it wrong and fail?

I've helped hundreds of authors process these fears and learn to make email a productive part of their marketing plan. If you wrestle with the concerns above, let me set the record straight:

It is impossible to over-communicate with your email subscribers, as long as you send value to the recipient.

Read that sentence above again. Let it sink in. Notice how it's plain common sense. If you send people an email that is interesting or helpful, they will not mind seeing another email from you again.

Most authors don't need to worry about over-communicating or offending. The real problem is communicating too rarely and risking obscurity. Yet, many authors get caught up in analysis-paralysis or procrastination, then fail to connect with their audience altogether.

I'm not suggesting that you adopt an email strategy that makes you uncomfortable. Let's be real. Anything you hate to do will never get done. I never force my author clients to do something that feels uncomfortable. But, how do you achieve the right balance between consistent communication and taking up too much of your time? The best answer is to send an email newsletter.

An "email newsletter" is an email that you send on a regular basis containing interesting information, updates, news, and promotions to buy your books. Suffice it to say, email newsletters are the least labor-intensive way to stay in touch with your subscribers and sell more books while you work on writing your next book. But, before I explain the details of creating an email newsletter, let me clear up a common misconception between subscribing to an author's blog versus subscribing to an author's email newsletter.

The Difference Between Blogging and Email Newsletters

Blogging can be an effective tool that works for a variety of authors. If you enjoy blogging, keep going. However, don't confuse writing a blog as a substitute for sending a regular email newsletter.

When you write a blog post, there is no guarantee that your entire audience will see it. Instead, you are relying on people to come to your author website to read your blog. Very few readers will do that on a consistent basis. So, most of your audience doesn't stay connected with you. They're out of the communication loop.

Can you ask people to subscribe to your blog by email? Sure, but that approach will handcuff your marketing efforts. It's unwieldy to insert an article, testimonials, event listings, personal updates, and a book promotion all into a single blog post. But, an email newsletter can simultaneously manage all of that information with ease. Thus, by asking people to only subscribe to your blog, you limit your ability to fully engage with your readers.

Blogging also represents a "passive" approach to marketing, because you rely on people come to you and read your updates. In contrast, email is an "active" marketing tactic, because you purposefully reach out to send updates and promotions to everyone on your list. The "active" nature of email newsletters makes it a superior choice over blogging - and social media as well.

If you're a novelist, sending weekly emails with self-help tips obviously isn't a good fit. But, that doesn't mean you should avoid emailing your audience for several months. How do you expect people to maintain interest in your books when you don't appear in their inbox for a long time? It's an arrogant mindset to believe people will jump to attention when you suddenly reappear. Frequency breeds familiarity. Familiarity breeds trust. Trust breeds book sales.

For example, I worked with a very successful novelist named Wanda Brunstetter, who has sold over 10 million copies of her Amish fiction stories. She's a big believer in email. Like clockwork, she sends a regular email newsletter to fans filled with updates, giveaways, contests, and light-hearted encouragement. If you write fiction, don't fall for the lie that email newsletters don't work for fiction. I'm sure you'd love to sell 10 million copies, too.

Another advantage of email over blogging is the ability to get real-time statistics, which means you can immediately judge the performance of campaign and get accurate data. Within hours after an email is sent, most email service providers can tell you how many people opened your emails, who opened your emails, and who clicked on the links you put inside. You don't have to wait for weeks to see if your emails are working.

Now that we're clear on the reasons why email newsletters make sense. Let's make sure you know how to create a news-letter that will motivate your subscribers to take action.

Create Scarcity Before You Hit "Send"

Did you know the average adult in America watches five hours of television per day? That's a lot of TV. Like me, you probably have a favorite program, so you make time to watch every episode that airs. However, there is an unspoken rule that comes with watching network television...you agree to watch the advertisements. You may not enjoy the ads, but you accept that trade-off in order to watch your favorite show.

Every television program includes commercials from companies who want you to buy their products. But, when those ads appear on your TV screen, do you get mad and stop watching your beloved show? No, you sit through the ads, absorb their messages, and return to watching your "free" television episode. The ads don't deter you from watching TV. Plus, if one of the commercials presents a product that is appealing, you may decide to buy it later that day, the next day, the next month, etc.

There is a silent agreement between television networks and TV viewers that all programs will come with advertising. It's part of the deal and everyone accepts this arrangement. When someone turns on their TV to watch a show, they expect to see advertising.

Your approach to email newsletters should be no different. There should also be a silent arrangement between and your subscribers that your emails will come with some advertising. Your emails will provide interesting and valuable content for free. But, there will also be ads to promote a new book, upcoming speaking events, spinoff products, backlist titles, etc.

Just like the television networks, you must set the proper expectation that your free content will also include advertising. If you set this assumption correctly, then both parties will experience a mutually beneficial cycle. If you don't, then either you or your subscribers will feel frustrated and avoid "tuning in."

Why do the proper expectations matter? There's an insidious problem that can occur with email newsletters if you set the wrong expectation:

You can train your subscribers to expect everything for free and never buy anything.

For example, let's imagine that I send you a weekly email newsletter filled with free articles or excerpts from my books. At the bottom of each newsletter, I display a picture of the book covers with some links to purchase at online retailers. I don't "push" the book. Instead, I let you decide to buy the book whenever you feel like it. If I repeat this process for an entire year, how many books do you think I'd sell?

The results would be limited because I'm letting you drive the purchasing process. Repeatedly sending free samples from my book with just a "silent" ask at the bottom of every email doesn't stir a big desire to purchase. You could argue that my book sales would be good if my samples are good. But, that idea is only partly true. Just because people like a free sample doesn't mean they'll immediately buy the book.

In most cases, people need a "reason" to buy. Good samples can act as a legitimate reason. But, the best way to get a person's attention is the "fear of missing out," also known as "FOMO." If you want your email subscribers to buy more books from you, create a sense of FOMO in their minds.

However, the problem with selling books is that they are always available. Anyone can purchase a book at anytime on Amazon and other retailers. Therefore, if people don't feel an immediate need to purchase your book, they can always sit on the fence and decide to buy later. That indecision can cost you a lot of lost book sales.

When a product is always available, you must overcome people's apathy by creating a reason to buy quickly. If you develop the fear of missing out, you can move people from feeling indifferent to feeling excited to buy. That process is within your control.

In other words, when you market a book without creating FOMO, it's like letting your customer drive the car. In contrast, when you create FOMO, then you take the steering wheel and drive the car. You always want to be in control of the sales process. If you market your book using a willy-nilly, hope-and-pray approach, then good luck selling many books.

Believe me, I learned this lesson the hard way. For several years, I sent a weekly email newsletter filled with free advice. At the bottom of each newsletter, I displayed a list of my books and products that subscribers could buy. It was a "silent" ask, because there was no focused sales pitch and no sense of urgency.

I regularly received compliments from my subscribers that they liked my newsletter content. But, I always felt disappointed with the overall sales. It seemed like I was doing a lot of work for minimal results.

Yet, the research studies that I saw kept touting the power of email marketing. Other people were claiming great results. So, I had to determine if the problem was email or if the problem was me. Since, I'm an imperfect human being, and I concluded that the problem probably started on my end.

Soon afterwards, I ran across a book called *Launch* by Jeff

Walker. Jeff's book hit #1 on the *New York Times* bestseller list, and he is known as the king of selling products online using email. As I read Jeff's book, I came across this quote:

To create a well-executed launch, you absolutely need to build scarcity into that launch. There has to be some negative consequence if people don't take action and buy before the end of the launch (for instance, the price might go up after the launch). If you make sure there's always some scarcity built into your launch, it will take your results to a completely different level.

Suddenly, the light bulb went off in my mind. Jeff was right. Scarcity is one of the keys to create the fear of missing out. If people think something good is about to disappear, they will naturally feel more motivated to take action.

However, most books can always be purchased on Amazon, so their availability is never scarce. This reality can put authors at a disadvantage when trying to generate new sales. Your email subscribers may never feel a sense of urgency. Therefore, people may tend to postpone their purchasing decision to a later time. Without scarcity or the fear of missing out, most people may never buy at all. How do you overcome this inertia?

Create something that is scarce, attach it to your book, and generate a new sense of urgency to purchase.

You can manufacture scarcity whenever you desire. Create something that people would want. Then, make that item disappear within a limited time, such as:

- Special low price
- Exclusive bonus content
- Unique bundle pack
- Chance to meet the author
- Contest to win prizes

When you attach an enticing incentive to your book that could soon vanish, you naturally heighten people's desire to buy your book. Now, you are in control of the sales process.

Here's a fun but useful example. There is a local doughnut shop where I live in Atlanta called Dutch Monkey Doughnuts. They make the absolute best doughnuts I've ever tasted. My favorite flavor is called "Chocolate Cream Pie." Sounds good, right? However, Dutch Monkey only makes Chocolate Cream Pie doughnuts on an occasional basis. Plus, they make their doughnuts in small batches, and their daily supply can run out by lunchtime. They frequently rotate flavors, so there can be several weeks when Chocolate Cream Pie isn't on the menu. Therefore, I never know when it will be available, so I feel a sense of scarcity about my favorite doughnut.

Therefore, every morning I go to Dutch Monkey's website and check their list of daily specials. If I see Chocolate Cream Pie on the list, I do a happy dance, then rush out of the house to buy some doughnuts before they're all gone. In other words, the basic principle of scarcity makes a grown man act like a fool just to buy a doughnut.

Dutch Monkey makes doughnuts every day of the year. You could say their product is a commodity. But, they heighten my desire to purchase by rotating an incentive for me to buy on a regular basis. They create artificial scarcity and generate a fear of missing out on my favorite doughnut.

How does eating doughnuts apply to sending email newsletters?

If you want to write newsletters that lead to book sales, then you must use newsletters to create artificial scarcity. You must lead your subscribers into feeling a heightened desire to purchase because something good is about to disappear. That incentive could be a lower price, bonus content, winning a prize, meeting the author, etc. Throughout the year, you should rotate these incentives for your book so that people regularly feel the need to purchase.

Before I realized the principle of scarcity, I used to randomly write articles for my newsletters, send them out, and hope people would buy my products. Even though I was consistent, this approach only produced minimal results and left me feeling frustrated.

I mistakenly assumed that "killing my subscribers with kindness" by giving away lots of free content would lead people to buy my products. The error of that mindset is that I put my subscribers in control of my sales. By enabling my subscribers to buy whenever they felt like it, I enabled their indifference and procrastination to rule the decision-making process.

Never let your book sales be ruled by the indifference or procrastination of others. You must take control of the sales process.

How do you take control of the book sales process? Use your email newsletter to stay engaged with your subscribers and create regular intervals of artificial scarcity.

The "Big Ask" Newsletter Approach

Take a moment to think about your favorite TV show. Notice that most of the content you watch is the program itself. But, a small amount of the content is the advertising. According to Nielsen data reported by the *Wall Street Journal*, most major networks run commercials around 25% of every hour. That's 15 minutes of ads for every 60 minutes. In other words, 75% of the programming is the free content. The other 25% is advertising.

A similar approach can work for your email newsletters. Send 75% of your newsletter content as free material that keeps subscribers engaged and happy. Then, send 25% of your newsletters to motivate people to buy your book using incentives and the principle of scarcity. I like to call this technique the "Big Ask" approach to newsletters.

Send email newsletters with free content that lead up to a "Big Ask" to buy your book.

The "Big Ask" approach to newsletters enables you to build interest and create a compelling reason to take action. People are more apt to purchase when you intensify their interest, give a compelling incentive to buy, and then remove that incentive. Removing the incentive creates a fear of missing out if people don't purchase during your "Big Ask."

Otherwise, people will remain on the fence and decide to buy down the road. You must remove that indifference.

Authors can offer a variety to incentives to motivate newsletter subscribers to take action, such as a special price, exclusive bonus, unique bundle pack, contest to win a prize, a chance to talk with the author, etc. Or, your "Big Ask" could be an exclusive webinar where you discuss your book in detail, take Q&A from people, and personally convince them to purchase. There must be a sense of scarcity involved during your "Big Ask." Otherwise, your newsletter subscribers will remain apathetic.

How do you develop a "Big Ask"? Use the same dynamic as the major TV networks. Place your email subscribers into a cycle of receiving your free newsletter with the agreement that you'll be advertising your products. But, you must strike the right balance between giving free content and advertising – similar to a TV show.

For instance, if your favorite show had a ridiculous amount of commercials, you'd get sick of watching no matter how much you liked the program. The same situation applies to email newsletters. You need to apply the right balance between giving versus asking. Typically, the 75/25 rule works best. Give 75% of the time. Ask 25% of the time.

The ideal way to use email newsletters is to run them like the season of a TV show. For example, the ultra-popular programs, such as *Survivor, Game of Thrones,* or *NCIS,* usually run a "season" of weekly episodes over a period of 2 – 3 months. Each weekly episode builds to a climax at the end of the season. After that culmination occurs, there is a short break. Then, another season of the show runs soon afterwards. The overall premise is the same, but the next series of episodes may focus on a different character, setting, or storyline. Yet, it's still the same program that you enjoy watching.

Likewise, an email newsletter can be effective when you organize the individual issues into a "season" of episodes like a TV show. Run a series of newsletters all based on the same book that builds to a "Big Ask." The "Big Ask" features a scarce incentive that motivates the desire to purchase. Once the campaign is over, then you run another "season" of newsletters that lead to a different "Big Ask."

You can create a "Big Ask" newsletter sequence by using these five steps:

Step 1 – Pick one of your books (or any other product) that you want to sell to your email subscribers.

Step 2 – Choose how long you want to promote this book to your email audience. A period of 4 – 8 weeks is typical.

Step 3 – Decide how frequently you wish to send your newsletters. Weekly is best, but once every two weeks is acceptable.

Step 4 – After you complete the three steps above, then determine how much content you need to fill each newsletter issue.

Each issue will include an article or excerpt around 500 – 800 words related to "Book X." The first 75% of your newsletter issues will give away free content without asking people to purchase. The last 25% of your newsletters will give away free content along with a "Big Ask" that highlights an incentive that will soon disappear. The incentive creates a sense of scarcity.

Step 5 – In most cases, it is wise to send one or two sales emails before and after your last newsletter issue to bring maximum awareness to the "Big Ask" and your disappearing incentive. These sales emails do not need to contain teaching content or book excerpts. They are brief reminders to your subscribers that your special incentive is about to vanish. Now is the time to act!

For example, let's say you pick "Book X" according to Step 1. In Step 2, you decide to promote "Book X" for 8 weeks. In Step 3, you decide to send newsletters on a weekly basis. Based on that math, you will send a total of 8 emails over an 8-week period. All eight emails will include a free excerpt or interesting content around 500 – 800 words related to "Book X." But, the first 75% of the newsletters (6 of the 8 total emails) will not ask for the sale. You will just be generous.

The last 25% of the newsletters, which are the final 2 of the 8 total emails, will offer free content and highlight your "Big Ask" to buy "Book X." Those last two emails generate the scarcity by calling attention to your incentive that will soon disappear, which could be a special discount, exclusive content, contest prize, Q&A with the author, etc.

Before and after email newsletter #8, you can include sending brief sales emails that remind people your incentive is about to go away. You can use attention-grabbing statements in your email subject line, such as:

Only 48 hours left...

Special discounts disappear on this date...

This is your last chance...

Don't miss out. Tomorrow it will be gone...

In many cases, the last 24 – 48 hours will produce the lion's share of the sales. That's because subscribers will genuinely feel a fear of missing out. The scarcity that you develop will create a sense of urgency that forces people to take action.

The "Big Ask" newsletter approach is designed to prevent authors from randomly writing articles and sending out issues on a haphazard basis. If you want to sell more books using email, it's better to create structure and scarcity to your campaigns. All that is required is a little forethought and planning, which will lead to better results.

For example, after I sent newsletters for years with random content that only got lackluster results, I decided to test the "Big Ask" method on myself. I put together a "season" of weekly newsletters over 6 weeks focusing on one of my products that costs $300. Obviously, $300 is a much higher price point than a $15 book, so there was a greater barrier to success. The first four weeks (75%) of my newsletters gave away free teaching articles that related to my $300 product with no ask to buy it. Then, the last two newsletters (25%) of the 6-week period gave away free content but focused on the "Big Ask" with scarcity. I also included two short sales emails at the end to remind everyone that time was running out.

Guess what happened? I made over $7,500 in sales at the end of my "Big Ask" campaign! In six weeks, I grossed more revenue than I had made in the past six months. However, I was concerned that this result might be an outlier. So, I repeated the same process for the same product a few months later. Guess what happened again? I achieved the same great result. After years of making measly revenue from my email newsletters, I made thousands of dollars in extra product sales in just a few months – simply by changing my approach.

Is the "Big Ask" method the only way to do author newsletters? No, there are authors who prefer to promote their books in a spontaneous fashion. Some authors, such as genre fiction, release new novels so frequently that each newsletter can focus on teasing and launching their next title. If those methods work for you, keep going with it.

However, I find that a haphazard approach to newsletters usually leads to nominal results. Your audience always takes their cue from you. Thus, when you focus your subscribers on one product and create a sense of scarcity, then you put yourself in the driver's seat of the sales process. That's the power of sending "Big Ask" newsletters.

Use the Circle of Engagement

Are you a non-fiction author who writes educational or inspirational articles for your newsletter? Take advantage of a time-saving benefit. Post your newsletter articles to your blog, if you have one, or add them to a free resources page on your author website. It's like killing two birds with one stone.

People who subscribe to your newsletter can read the articles. And, people who visit your website can enjoy the same content. Plus, you may have email subscribers who would like to re-read some of your past newsletter articles. By posting them on your website, they are always available for anyone to access.

If you use social media, you can take your content one step further. When you post a newsletter article to your blog, place a message on your social media accounts with a teaser and a link to that blog article. This step helps drive traffic from your social media audience to your author website where they can read your content. When people visit your author website to read your blog, they'll see an offer to get your content magnet and join your email newsletter. Now, they're on your email list. Pretty ingenious, eh?

My friend and website wizard, Eddy Pareja, at Sangfroid Web Design (https://www.SangfroidWebDesign.com) calls this clever sequence, "The Circle of Engagement." When you write an article for your newsletter, use it in three different ways.

First, send the article to your email subscribers to read in a newsletter.

Second, post that article to your blog for website visitors to read. The more articles you post to your blog, the more ways people can find your website during a Google search.

Third, direct people from your social media pages to read the same article on your blog.

As people visit your blog from social media or a Google search to read the article, you can lead them to join your email list by displaying a free content magnet as described in Chapter 2. Using this process, more people will become all-important email subscribers. It's like watching your marketing efforts come full circle. The "Circle of Engagement" saves time and creates multiple benefits simply by writing one good article.

What If You Only Have One Book or Write Fiction?

When I consult with first-time authors, some wonder how the "Big Ask" newsletter approach can work if they only have one book to sell. In addition, some novelists wonder how to use the approach if they write fiction at a slow pace. How do you give away excerpts from the same book over a long time period?

In situations where you have limited content, you may only conduct a "Big Ask" campaign 2 – 3 times a year for a few weeks at a time. In between those campaigns, you switch to sending newsletters that focus on a different type of content:

Write newsletters that sell who you are as a writer or an expert.

Besides selling your books, you can also share the interesting parts of who you are as an author. If you write non-fiction, reveal more facets of your expertise that may not be expressed within your books. Use these questions to spark ideas for newsletter articles:

- What are the most common questions that I get from my readers?
- What are the most common problems that my audience faces?
- What have I learned in the past month that would benefit my readers?

If you write fiction, open up about the fun or stressful aspects of being a novelist. Weave other parts of your life into your newsletters. Talk about the process of being an author, share other areas of know-how, or give a behind the scenes look into your everyday life.

In her book, *Newsletter Ninja*, Tammy Labrecque encourages authors to insert these types of personal elements into their newsletters:

Also, keep in mind that anything you send that's relevant to you and your work—especially cover reveals, sneak peeks, and the like—is a powerful form of selling without selling. Hyping up your work by letting subscribers in on the creative process, in large or small ways, gets them excited.

Also, book recommendations, funny memes, cool research, travel diaries, pet pictures, etc. If you're constantly delivering laughs, great recommendations, or whatever it is that your subscribers love, they're going to tell their friends "You've got to sign up for this; it's awesome."

If you don't have enough content from one book to create a

"season" of newsletters that leads to a "Big Ask," then pull content from your life. Most of your subscribers are interested in the writing routine of being an author or a peek at your regular day. Remember, your email subscribers are your fans. They may like your book, but they also like you. Give them more of you. For instance, you could create a newsletter issue using the ideas below:

- Share examples or stories of how you conduct research for your book
- Share a behind the scenes look at your writing life, office, or writing method
- Share your favorite book, movie, or app recommendations
- Share your favorite travel tips or places to visit
- Insert your favorite recipes or music playlists
- Add links to recent articles or news headlines you find fascinating

For example, business author and *New York Times* bestseller, Dan Pink, has over 150,000 email subscribers. He sends out his popular "PinkCast" newsletter every other week. Within each issue, Dan includes three things that recently caught his attention, such as book recommendations, favorite movies, time-saving tools, insightful quotations, etc. Then, he always includes a 90-second video with tips for working smarter or living better. Dan's fans love his personal touch.

If you only have one book or write fiction, you may also wonder about how to create scarcity and boost response during your "Big Ask" campaign. Below are several options to create a sense of urgency for a new novel or a title you've written in the past. You could offer these incentives for a limited time that vanish by a certain date:

- Price discount
- Free prequel to the novel you're selling
- Free novella or side story about a key character from a novel
- Offer readers a chance to "Write yourself into my story" where readers can get their name inserted as a character into your book or novella
- Chance to win a private phone call with the author

It doesn't matter if you write fiction or only have one book available, a consistent newsletter approach can still produce results. The difference is that you may need to create more content about yourself because pulling content from your book will be limited. That balance is up to you.

When executed correctly, the "Big Ask" newsletter approach will build people's desire to buy to a crescendo. That crescendo ends with a focused opportunity to purchase your book. At that time, you offer a compelling incentive to purchase, such as an attractive price discount, exclusive bonus, or a packaged bundle with related products. The options are endless.

As described earlier, email newsletters work best when organized like the season of a TV show. You build for several weeks to the crescendo of subscribers purchasing one product. You enjoy the sales from that crescendo. Then, you start over the next week and start building towards a crescendo for a different product. Or, you can switch gears for a few issues and send newsletters that feature your life or expertise as an author.

You can repeat this process throughout the year for new books or backlist books. You can run a newsletter "season" for 4 weeks, 6 weeks, 12 weeks, etc. In addition, you can use the process to promote other products besides your books, such as a video course, paid webinar, live event, subscription program, training service, etc.

Energize your email subscribers to buy your products by using a series of related newsletters to heighten their interest. Rather than send indiscriminate newsletters that are unrelated to each other, use the "Big Ask" approach to lead people down a logical purchasing path.

8

NEWSLETTER FORMATTING TIPS

When you're ready to create an email newsletter, most reputable email service providers offer easy to use templates within their system. (Refer back to Chapter 4 for a review of email service providers). Using a template saves time and makes it simple to create professional-looking newsletters. Once you choose a template and send your first issue, you can reuse the same layout again in the future. Just make a copy of the previous newsletter layout and insert new content into the same template.

As you get comfortable loading content into your newsletter template, use these formatting tips to maintain a consistent and effective appearance:

Create Subject Lines that Grab Attention and Build Trust

Most people will ignore your newsletter if the subject line looks boring or suspicious. So, getting people to open your email is an important step. One way to tackle this challenge is to create an attention-grabbing subject line. For example, which of the two subject lines below look more appealing and credible?

- WEEKLY NEWSLETTER: Open Right Away!
- Rob Eagar's Monday Marketing Minute: "The Future of Publishing"

The first subject line looks dubious with the letters screaming at you in all caps along with a pushy request to "Open Right Away!" In addition, the text is too generic. People who see an ambiguous subject line like this example will ignore it or delete it.

The second subject line is an example from my popular weekly email newsletter for authors. My name helps generate credibility. The phrase "Monday Marketing Minute" lets recipients know what to expect. And, the attention-grabbing title, "The Future of Publishing" creates curiosity that moves people to open my email.

Likewise, your newsletter open rate will increase if you create a consistent name for your newsletters that subscribers quickly recognize. Below are several examples of email newsletter subject lines that establish consistency and interest in the minds of recipients:

The Marriage Minute from John Gottman

DeVon Franklin's - Mentor Mail

Dan Pink's - Pinkcast Newsletter

Alan Weiss - The Balancing Act E-Newsletter

Lisa Morrone's - Monday Morning Health Tip

The Getting the Love You Want Newsletter

Dr. Henry Cloud's - Boundaries Newsletter

The 5 Love Languages Newsletter

Kim Miller's - Boundaries for Your Soul Newsletter

Clark Sense with Clark Howard

If the open rate for your newsletter drops below the industry average of 17%, the culprit might be ineffective subject lines. Experiment with different types of subject lines that are more enticing. Some email service providers will let you split test different subject lines to find the best option before sending a newsletter to your entire list.

Keep Newsletter Articles Brief

The content that you create for a newsletter issue can come from different sources. As mentioned in the previous chapter, when you create a newsletter "season" that leads to a "Big Ask," pull excerpts or write articles directly related to your book. When you aren't focused on selling a specific product, write articles that sell who you are as a writer or an expert.

But, no matter how you create the content, keep the article length brief. Most email subscribers are not in the mood to read a long article on a tiny computer screen or a mobile device. For most "feature articles" within a newsletter, I recommend a typical length of 500 – 800 words.

However, there may be times with a longer article is necessary, such as 1,000 words or more. In that case, insert the first 3 – 4 paragraphs of your feature article into your email newsletter template. Make the last sentence end with a provocative teaser to keep reading. Then, display a link to your author website or blog to read the rest of the article in its entirety. Post all of the article on your website. Then, at the end of your blog post, display links to the webpage or retailer where people can buy the book related to your article.

Promote Your Book at the Top of an Email

Whenever you use email to promote a book, always display information about that book at the top of your email. For example, you might send a newsletter that includes a feature article or other information for subscribers to read. But, here's a little-known secret about email marketing:

Whatever people see at the top of an email newsletter gets the most attention. Whatever people see at the bottom of an email newsletter gets the least attention.

This fact was proven to me when I consulted on a project with a division of HarperCollins Publishers. During the project, I was hired to write over a year's worth of email newsletters based on content from a popular series of books. The email newsletter service we used at the time was an expensive system developed by IBM. One of the features in this system was the ability to track which links received the most clicks within an email.

As I reviewed the data from a year's worth of email newsletters, a consistent pattern emerged. The links posted at the top of an email newsletter received a lot more clicks than the content at the bottom of the newsletter. The difference was noticeable. Plus, it made common sense.

When you put something at the top of an email newsletter, you know that anyone who opens your newsletter will see it. Everyone reads emails from top to bottom. In contrast, not everyone who opens your newsletter will scroll down to the lower parts, especially the very bottom. Whatever you put at the top is guaranteed to be seen. But, that's not the case for content placed further down in the layout.

Therefore, if you want to use email newsletters to boost your book sales – put a promotion for your book at the top of your newsletter. I know this step may sound counterintuitive or overtly promotional. But, if you display your book at the middle or bottom of your newsletter, you risk many people never seeing that it exists.

When you promote a book at the top of your email newsletter, be sure to display an image of the front cover art. Place the picture into the top section of your email template along with concise marketing copy about your book.

If your promoting a novel, start your descriptive text with a marketing hook and provide a brief synopsis of the most emotional or suspenseful part of your story. Then, close with a cliffhanger question or statement.

If you're promoting a non-fiction book, start the marketing text with an attention-grabbing hook then briefly explain the results that readers will receive. List the benefits as bulleted points to make the information easy for people to read on a small mobile device screen.

For details on writing marketing hooks and sizzling book descriptions, see my book, *The Author's Guide to Write Text That Sells Books*.

Underneath the marketing text, display purchase links to the major online retailers, such as Amazon, Barnes & Noble, iBooks, or IndieBound. Unless you have chosen to only sell your books through Amazon, it's best to give links to more than one retailer to avoid playing favorites.

Enhance Your Credibility with Endorsements or Reader Reviews

There is nothing that you can say about yourself that is as powerful as what happy readers say about you. Try as you may to create clever marketing text, most people give more credence to what their peers might say about your book. That's why your email newsletter should regularly include an endorsement, testimonial, success story, or positive reader review.

In most cases, display endorsements or reader reviews underneath your book promotion and feature article sections in your newsletter layout. They don't require top billing, but they can provide a powerful credibility boost when seen in the middle of your newsletter by subscribers.

If you're just starting out as an unknown author, copy and paste a 5-star Amazon or GoodReads review about your book. Or, if you received an email from a happy fan who enjoyed your book, paste their positive comment into this section of your newsletter layout. The goal is to display any public praise you have available and use it to build your authority.

If you're a more experienced author, rotate endorsements from well-known leaders, industry reviews, testimonials, or success stories. Keep the endorsement brief to just 1 – 3 sentences. Your subscribers care more about who says the words than how many words are said. If you have permission to use the endorser's picture, insert a head shot image for an added touch.

Use the power of other people praising your book. When someone else says something good about your book, it speaks louder than anything you can say yourself.

Break Up the Monotony with Interviews or Guest Posts

Occasionally, you may hit "writer's block" when trying to create articles for your email newsletter. Here's an option that I recommend as a last resort or when you need fresh content. Interview someone else as a special guest, or recruit another author to write a "guest post."

Asking another author to contribute content is a great way to save time and spice up your newsletters. Plus, you're doing that author a favor by giving him or her exposure to your audience. Many people will jump at the chance to gain access to a new audience. And, your subscribers won't care if the material doesn't come from you – as long as it's considered helpful information. Just don't use this option too often, or people will assume you're not really an expert.

If you solicit guest posts, maintain control over the content and tone of any articles. You want the outside contributor to feel like a natural fit for your readers. Clarify the type of articles and topics that you prefer for your email newsletters. Review all submissions and make revisions before sending them out to your subscribers.

You may find it easier to create a list of article topics that guest writers can use as a guide. Then, put out a call for submissions whenever you need new content or feel pressed for time, such as working on a manuscript deadline or going on vacation.

Or, you could create an article based on a written interview, where you supply the questions and the guest sends back written answers. You can engage with the guest by email or in an actual interview by audio or video.

Keep your email newsletter professional and interesting by using the tips in this chapter. Maximize your subject lines and keep articles brief. Always place your book promotions at the top where everyone can see them. Enhance your credibility with endorsements. And, reach out to other authors for guest posts or interviews if you hit newsletter "writer's block."

CONCLUSION

There are many aspects of an author's life that can feel beyond your control, such as wishing for a national television interview, working with an apathetic publisher, trying to locate new readers, or hoping to get more Amazon reviews. Sometimes, this lack of control can make you question why you decided to become an author in the first place.

I wrote this book to help you take back your power. Nothing puts the control into your hands quite like email marketing. When you amass a large email list, you gain greater ability to directly influence your book sales. Publishers, agents, and other authors also view you more favorably. In summary, email puts you in a position of strength.

It is my desire that you use this book to wield the power of email in your favor. As we discussed earlier:

- Email marketing is vastly superior to social media at selling books directly to your fans.

- Email is less expensive and more productive than other marketing channels.
- Email enables you to directly engage and maintain influence with readers.
- Email can be tracked to determine performance in real-time.
- Email works regardless of whether you write fiction or non-fiction.
- Email is beneficial to first-time authors as well as established bestsellers.
- Email is effective at marketing new books and backlist titles.

However, email will only work as long as you make it a priority of your marketing efforts. Converting new subscribers into book sales doesn't happen by itself. But, I like to close with good news:

There is nothing stopping you from succeeding with email marketing.

No one can prevent you from offering enticing content magnets, attracting new subscribers, creating an automated onboard sequence, sending persuasive sales emails, and delivering value-laden newsletters. It's all within your control.

Every author feels a sense of relief when they finish writing a book. But, I want you to feel a sense of excitement about selling your book. I hope the advice within these pages empowers you to reach your goals both now and long into the future.

I wish you all the best on your author journey. As you apply the principles in this book and experience success with email marketing, please do me a favor: send me an email!

Rob@RobEagar.com

To your success,

Rob Eagar

Make an Author Happy Today

If you found the material in this book helpful, I'd be eternally grateful if you took a few minutes to write a review on Amazon.

When you leave a comment on Amazon, the world's largest bookseller, it makes a huge difference to help new readers find my books.

Your review would make my day!

Thank you

MY FREE GIFT FOR YOU

Get three e-books to help jumpstart your book sales for FREE:

Find Readers and Sell Books on a Shoestring Budget

Mastering Book Hooks for Authors

The Ultimate Book Marketing Plan Template for Authors

Join my email newsletter and get these three e-books. Each resource can be downloaded as a file to your computer or added to any e-reader device. You will also receive my weekly e-newsletter packed with free expert marketing advice for authors.

Download these three e-books for free today at:

https://www.startawildfire.com/free-ebooks-ag

ABOUT ROB EAGAR

Rob Eagar is a marketing consultant and one of the most accomplished book marketing experts in America. He has coached over 450 authors, advised top publishing houses, provided industry intelligence, and created instructional resources for writers. Highlights from Rob's consulting work with clients include:

- Helped books hit the *New York Times* bestseller list three different ways
- Built and expanded email lists by over 25,000 subscribers in nine months
- Rebranded multiple authors who became *New York Times* bestsellers
- Designed numerous author websites that doubled visitor traffic within 60 days
- Developed bestselling book titles, marketing hooks, and book descriptions
- Revived a backlist book to hit the *New York Times* bestseller list after 23 years in print

Rob founded Wildfire Marketing, a consulting practice that has attracted numerous bestselling authors, including Dr. Gary Chapman, DeVon Franklin, Lysa TerKeurst, Wanda Brunstetter, Harville Hendrix, and Dr. John Townsend. In addition, he's consulted with imprints of the world's best-known publishers, such as HarperCollins (Thomas Nelson, Zondervan), Hachette (FaithWords), Simon & Schuster

(Howard Books) and numerous small to mid-sized publishers.

Rob's expertise stems from starting out as a successful multi-published author. In 2002, he self-published his first book and generated a consistent six-figure income, long before the rise of social media and Amazon. His book was later purchased by a traditional publisher, sold over 50,000 copies, and remained on bookstore shelves for over 10 years.

His success attracted the attention of other authors who sought out Rob for marketing advice. This led him to found Wildfire Marketing in 2007 and provide marketing education to authors around the world. In addition, Rob partnered with Writer's Digest to publish the book, *Sell Your Book Like Wildfire*, and teach his online video course, *Mastering Amazon for Authors*.

Rob's industry-leading instruction can now be found in *The Author's Guide* series, a collection of books dedicated to teaching critical marketing topics, including:

The Author's Guide to Marketing Books on Amazon

The Author's Guide to Write Text That Sells Books

The Author's Guide to Email Marketing

Rob has served as a contributing writer and educator for Book Business Magazine, Digital Book World, Writer's Digest, and Reedsy. His national media appearances include interviews on the CBS Early Show, CNN Radio, and the *Los Angeles Times*. His background includes a marketing degree from Auburn University and 10 years of corporate sales experience before working full-time in publishing.

Rob is married to Ashley the Wonderful. When he isn't consulting, you can find Rob fly-fishing for monster trout, breaking 40mph on his road bike, or loudly playing his drums. Ashley would prefer that he join her to quietly paint, work in their garden, or watch Jane Austen movies. They reside near Atlanta, Georgia. For more details about Rob, his books, and his consulting services, visit his website at:

http://www.RobEagar.com

GET EXPERT HELP FOR YOUR BOOKS

Are you're tired of trying to figure out book marketing by yourself? What if an experienced coach guided you to the next level? Get personal help from one of the most accomplished experts in America:

Book Marketing Master Class

You can master your book sales. It's not a dream. The Book Marketing Master Class teaches how to master all key aspects of marketing a book. Whether you're a first-time author or a seasoned bestseller, Rob Eagar will show you how to:

- Attract more readers using the power of free content and email.
- Create persuasive language, including hooks, titles, and back cover copy.
- Construct a complete marketing plan to maximize the book launch sequence.
- Turn your author website into a book-selling machine.
- Maximize inexpensive advertising on Amazon and Facebook.
- Connect with online influencers and turn media interviews into book sales.
- Discover multiple ways to create new income from your book content.

Rob's expertise applies to fiction and non-fiction, first-timer or bestseller, indie author or traditionally-published. He will personally teach you his proven marketing techniques and apply his instruction to your specific books, goals, and experience level. Work with Rob in person or receive instruction via live video sessions. Include your team and get everyone coached up at the same time. Receive follow-up access to ask Rob questions, hold you accountable, and request his review of your work. For details, visit:

https://www.startawildfire.com/consulting/book-marketing-master-class

Personal 90-Minute Author Coaching Sessions

Are your book sales stagnant? Got a nagging marketing or publishing question? Ready to raise the bar on your author career? Reach your goals by talking directly with a world-class expert. Schedule a personal 90-minute author coaching session with Rob Eagar.

Individual coaching sessions include direct access to Rob to ask questions and learn how to improve your book marketing skills. Using live video screenshare technology, he will walk you step-by-step through everything you need to know. Get immediate answers to reach more readers, build a larger audience, sell more books, and increase your author revenue. For details, visit:

https://www.startawildfire.com/consulting/author-consultation

OTHER BOOKS BY ROB EAGAR

The Author's Guide to Write Text That Sells Books

The Author's Guide to Marketing Books on Amazon

For more information, visit:

http://www.RobEagar.com

Printed in Great Britain
by Amazon